HOPE FOR THE CAVEMAN

Becoming New Men for Today's World

Patrick Williams, MD

iUniverse, Inc.
Bloomington

Hope for the Caveman
Becoming New Men for Today's World

iUniverse books may be ordered through booksellers or by contacting:

iUniverse
1663 Liberty Drive
Bloomington, IN 47403
www.iuniverse.com
1-800-Authors (1-800-288-4677)

Because of the dynamic nature of the Internet, any web addresses or links contained in this book may have changed since publication and may no longer be valid. The views expressed in this work are solely those of the author and do not necessarily reflect the views of the publisher, and the publisher hereby disclaims any responsibility for them.

ISBN: 978-1-4620-2775-0 (sc)
ISBN: 978-1-4620-2774-3 (hc)
ISBN: 978-1-4620-2773-6 (e)

Library of Congress Control Number: 2011909710

Printed in the United States of America

iUniverse rev. date: 06/29/2011

TABLE OF CONTENTS

PREFACE
(Note from the Author)

Having practiced medicine, Internal and Geriatric, for twenty-five years, I have become increasingly aware of the problems men face in our time. Why are men so confused about their roles, what to do and how to act, young *and* old? Why is our brotherhood so punctuated by disorientation? Where did our compass go, why did we lose it, and how do we get it back? It's no wonder men are so misunderstood by *women*, when so few of us actually understand *ourselves*.

A life-long love affair with self-discovery, combined with the daily presentation of "lost" men to my practice, led me down the path of this book. Stimulated to study the problem not only as a personal quest for my own answers but also eventually out of response to what has become an over-arching issue in our society, I found a wealth of information on the critical losses men have suffered as a result of these issues. I believe that I have been able to piece together what the essential needs of men are if we hope to become mature and productive. It expands beyond the fact that we need to hear that we are not "wrong" in our nature. More than that, we need a path and we need a structure in which to understand ourselves if we are to flourish as men in today's and tomorrow's world.

Let me share a story that demonstrates some of the casualties I have personally suffered in my life as a result of this dilemma.

I began my medical training in 1980. The system of medical training was onerous to say the least. It was a strict male-designed model. The expectations were: extremely long hours, on call all night as much as every other night, no family life, wife and children unattended in favor of medicine, and most of all – no whining. It was designed with an outcome in mind. This outcome was to be the best physician possible. It was designed to have future physicians make the fewest mistakes by having the most experience possible before leaving training. The more one was on duty, the less "learning opportunities" were missed. It was painful but men considered this a badge of honor. Sleep deprivation and exhaustion were part and parcel to the business. Family life was difficult at best.

During seven years of training I spent two hours a day with my family. I would come home for a "family dinner" during which I would solicit how the children's day went and exchange any information with my wife that was needed to run the household. I would then return to the library or anatomy lab until at least midnight or to be being on call all night. On the nights I came home, I would rise at 5 A.M. to go to my research job so I could make a contribution to the family income. My wife was, of necessity, expected to deal with all household and children-related problems. While I could play the role of "involved father" at dinner, I did not really have the time or energy to be emotionally involved in their lives. This came back to bite me later on as it had with so many physicians before me.

Driven by these factors, at the time of my training and for some time after, the suicide rate for physicians was the highest of any profession or occupation. It was apparently more honorable to die than to admit one couldn't stand the pressure. We still lose four hundred physicians a year in the United States to suicide, predominantly men. (*Web MD*, "Physician Suicide", Updated March 29, 2010) The prevalence of alcohol and drug abuse among physicians was also the highest of any job. It was estimated that the rate of active substance abuse was from eight to twelve percent among physicians. (*Hospital Physician*, "Substance Abuse Among Physicians: What You Need To Know", July 2003). Divorce rates were astronomical. Thankfully the rate has fallen from a peak of forty-four percent in 1987 to thirty-seven percent today. (*National Review of Medicine*, March 15, 2006, Vol. 3, No. 5)

In my own way I thought I was doing the right thing. I thought I was loving my family. I was preparing to be the best "provider" I could be. I was failing miserably at it.

The traditional system of medical training had been based on the young-adult style of the male brain. But the system was designed, supported and enforced by a hierarchy of elder men who weren't making the transition to wisdom leaders. They weren't seeing the forest for the trees. Ironically, as data began to come out that sleep deprivation and exhaustion were resulting in more errors, rather than better training, the system was pressured into a more humane schedule. Thankfully, training now has evolved to honor family and a life outside of medicine.

I, as a typical man, accepted this training without question. It was a "privilege" to be mentored by these men. With blinders on, I didn't understand or had lost track of what was going to lead to long-term happiness for myself and my family. It was with this understanding, and the realization that there are countless other men suffering similar casualties every day, that I was motivated to write this book. Showing young men the way to responsible manhood, helping middle-aged men make the transition to most useful and fulfilling second part of life possible, and challenging older men to step into the role of mentoring elders is what this book is about. It has been part of my transition to second adulthood.

PRELUDE

Perhaps the following illustration will throw into sharp relief the impact our lack of awareness of our true nature has—not only on ourselves as men, but on our relationships as well, magnifying the confusion we all, both men and women, experience in our lives:

A man and a woman are enjoying a wonderful meal at a restaurant. He is looking deeply into her eyes as they have a delightful and intimate conversation. The relationship is promising everything each of them could want from the other. They get up and leave the restaurant. On exiting the door, he suddenly becomes quiet. She continues the conversation as they walk to the car. But something has changed. He is no longer looking at her or paying attention. She is confused at this sudden shift. *Is it my perfume? Does he see another woman he found more interesting? Did I forget to say thank you?* By the time they are both in the car and he has gotten the car out of the parking lot and heading home, he is ready to resume the conversation and attempts to do so. She is confused and possibly angry. If his apparent mood can shift that quickly, what can she expect from him? She doesn't understand. She doesn't feel secure in the relationship now. *He* doesn't understand her new, less than loving attitude, when a moment ago they were so mutually, pleasurably engaged. *Is it my breath? Did I forget my deodorant? Should I have opened her door?* They arrive at her house. He doesn't know what to expect. *Shall I try to kiss her? Will she invite me in?* There is tension between them but neither understands why. They fumble through a parting and both leave the evening shaking their heads. What happened?

Studies have shown that the differences in the way our brains work make men scan the environment for danger without consciously being aware of it, while women continue to focus on the relationship above all. This unconscious behavior may be antiquated in men and they are most often totally unaware that they are doing it, but it is still there, built in by eons of evolution. It is only a brief interlude – the transition from the restaurant to the car – from safe place to safe place – but the misunderstanding of what's happening leads to profound confusion, disappointment and the loss of opportunity for relationship. Not surprisingly, we have continued to linger in the untruth that we are somehow confounding one another - driving each other crazy - on purpose. Actually, we are desperately trying to show love for one another. It is misconstrued because we do not understand the genetic differences in the way we think, perceive and value. Moreover, our culture has reinforced the thought that female behavior is the ideal and thus has led us into the myth of male behavior as substandard. This has resulted in the dilution of masculinity, and for this the world has suffered. Let me explain.

INTRODUCTION

Brain research from the last few decades has rapidly expanded our knowledge of the mechanisms of the human brain. With the publication of *Brain Sex* in 1989, *S/he Brain* in 1996 and finally *Male/Female* in 1998, scientists of both genders have passed this information into the public domain – but *not* into the public's awareness. Males and females think, see, hear, and feel differently from birth. Male and female brains are designed differently. They are intended for different primary purposes. They preferentially attend to different things. They tend to value different things. They perceive the world, and what is important in it, significantly differently. These differences in perception are so profound that they interfere with communication between males and females.

These differences resulted from millions of years of evolution, guided by natural selection, for our species survival. During this time we were hunters and gathers. We were *designed* for hunting and gathering well before the modern age, before civilization as we know it. This period of being hunters and gatherers far outstrips in length the modern era – millions versus thousands of years. For this reason, the respective ways of seeing things designed to facilitate those roles are still with us. These differences have served us all well as a species but we are in an age now where we want to deny these differences. In some ways they may be outdated, but that does not mean that they do not exist.

We really would like for them to be cultural, and therefore malleable to public opinion. Many of us still believe that everything is and should be the same for all of us, male and female. This thought is a well-defended axiom of our culture now. We want this to be true because it would be so much easier for people to change behavior, if it were all a cultural phenomenon. If only all the differences in the way men and women think and act were determined *after* birth. If only the way we were raised, the toys we were given, the games we were allowed to play, determined how we thought and felt, what we wanted to do, and how we communicated. But it's *not* true. It's *not* that simple. We have been desperately trying to train boy's behavior out of them for years in subtle and not so subtle ways. However, boy behavior was built in for a reason. We need to accept it and embrace it as "what is", based on what "has been". It is part of the structure and function of our brains.

The problem is bigger than playing and learning, dating and mating, working and loving. It is bigger than action versus talking. Men and women have begun outliving the bodies and brains that we were given by successful evolution. The way our brains are designed may pose a greater dilemma for men than for women. Fortunately, the women's movement has freed us from role expectation and society is attempting to point the way for men. Unfortunately, this same culture has turned upside down the phrase from *Pygmalion:* "Why can't a woman be more like a man." Men are often considered "immature" and "insensitive" – the standard being more like a woman. We must overcome this mythology of maleness as pathology - overcome the myth that if only we were more like women, the world would be a better place - overcome the idea that we *should* be more like women, if we only tried, if we only *cared*. What we *must* understand is that the world became a better place *because* we are who we are – because of who we evolved to be. Our gifts of perception have been as valuable to the species survival as those with which women have been gifted. They are not going to change any time soon. While, no doubt, we are still evolving, it is a slow process.

How can we best use our natural gifts to be of service to the world and mankind?

First we must recognize our way of being *as* a *gift*, to us and to the greater good. We must understand and accept ourselves as we are, as a starting place. Only *then* can we embrace the adjustments that will facilitate our growth and evolution.

The explosion of research on the human brain anatomy, physiology, and neurochemistry has finally not only revealed and defined the vast differences in the male and female of the species, but the behavior patterns associated with these differences. As a society, we have historically always known that men and women were different. Unfortunately, we have just been in denial lately. Now that we know the hows and the whys with more and more accuracy, we can begin to work with them.

First, we have to admit that these differences are real – that they exist – that they are *hard-wired*. The tendency of American culture over the last fifty years has been to emphasize the opposite.

I believe that as men, we are not living out of our full potential to be as useful, as creative, or as productive as we can be, until we embrace our masculinity, responsibly. Living a lie, denying who we are, is never a path to authenticity. I believe that society suffers as a result. The models that boys and young men see are often not very attractive. Older men are trying to emulate them, instead of the other way around. The ethics and morals we exhibit are self-serving. We worship money. We worship the immature, self-aggrandizing sports and cultural stars. Our responsibilities to the young have been abandoned in our rush to perpetuate ourselves in eternal youth. We have left them rudderless in a dangerous age. A pack of adolescent males, left to their own devices, is a scary sight for any society. That's often what our society looks like – a pack of adolescents, of various ages, acting with impunity. Society thirsts for an authentic male presence. Where are the elders - the elders that hold accountability and integrity as their creed?

The beauty of the women's movement is that it not only freed up women to be all they can be, but it has freed up men, as well, from reactive role identification. Men are now free to use the information science has given us to stop feeling guilty, to quit blaming ourselves, and to break the fetters of role *playing* without understanding.

The state of masculine spirit in today's America is in sad shape. It is no one else's responsibility to reclaim it. Indeed, no one else can. We have been taught to cultivate our feminine. We are perfectly capable of doing so and the effort is not a waste of time. The problem comes when this cultivation comes with the denial of our masculinity. Unfortunately, the culture has suggested, and we have *accepted*, the idea that feminine values are better than those inherent to men. The pendulum has swung too far. We are raised with this subtle message. "Boy" behavior is bad. "Girl" behavior is good. This loss of recognition of the masculine energy's value not only is sucking the marrow out of our souls, but it is doing grave injury to our society. The value we have to offer our wives, our sons and daughters, our fathers, our brothers and society at large, is greatly diminished by this de-masculinization. Reclaiming a sense of pride in who we are, placing the sacred masculine up there beside the sacred feminine, serves us all better. It is in fact essential if we are to survive. We need to assert ourselves. We need to focus not on what is wrong with us but on what is *right* with us. God made us who we are. It would be a sin to deny it.

PART ONE:

UNDERSTANDING THE EVOLUTIONARY BLUEPRINT

CHAPTER ONE:
THE NAKED APE

Why are we the way we are? What determined our biology? Why does biology rule?

Before I assume that we all possess the same body of knowledge on the evolution of the human species and how that explains our current nature, let me lay the groundwork for our understanding of these differences in the modern male and female brain. Why would the male and female human brain evolve differently?

Desmond Morris

"There are one hundred and ninety-three living species of monkeys and apes. One hundred ninety-two of them are covered with hair. The exception is a naked ape self-named *Homo sapiens*." So starts Desmond Morris's 1967 seminal work *The Naked Ape*. He goes on to say "… in acquiring lofty new motives, he has lost none of the earthy old ones." To further elucidate this statement is the next intention of this book.

In summarizing the research on our species up to that time and brilliantly speculating on their correlation with modern human behavior, Desmond Morris introduced much of the public to the field of anthropology. (He was still calling himself a zoologist.) Follow me as I remind us all of Morris' theses.

He pointed out, substantiated by field work on skeletal findings, that our ancestral apes evolved from smaller high tree dwelling species

1

to larger low-lying branch-swinging species and finally to the ground. In order to survive they had to compete with other ground dwellers. They had to become either better hunters than old-time carnivores or better grazers than old-time herbivores. The exploitation of the plant life on the African savannah was severely limited. The digestive system necessary for the direct use of the grassland was lacking. Apes and humans can't digest grass for nutrition. The great ancestral apes were, however, already omnivores. Animal protein had long become a necessarily important part of their diet as they supplemented their fruit with insects and small tree-dwelling reptiles, birds and mammals. Adaptation, for our ancestors, took the form of increasing this aspect of their diet. To thrive, natural selection moved toward making them better hunters. Protein, with its incorporation of fat, in a society that wasn't threatened by obesity but rather by starvation, led to a higher percentage of surviving members, especially the more vulnerable pregnant woman and children who, once they reached the ground, didn't obtain it as easily.

A Natural Progression

The evolving hominids already had good hands for grasping. As the brain developed and evolved, tool use was born. Next, the occipital lobes of the brain grew massively to enhance man's eyesight as his main hunting sense. An ability to "see" in three dimensions evolved, to facilitate hunting. We will later identify this as spatial relations. He could not only sense movement with his new, bigger and better visual lobes but he could gauge relative speed and angles of pursuit with his ability to "see" or think in three dimensions.

Early man, as primates, already had some degree of social organization. It was natural to develop as pack hunters, using their superior brains, to outwit the solitary hunters of their era. With their better cognitive ability they developed more sophisticated levels of cooperation and communication. How the brain was organized as it grew was made to support these functions as we will see.

Early hominids stood and walked upright. This freed their hands for tool and weapon use, even while moving about or eventually running. The angle of the spine and pelvis changed and the posture became more upright. The legs became longer and the speed increased. Running and running long distances developed. Humans developed the ability to breathe through their mouths, to pant, as they ran. While they weren't as fast as prey animals on the plains of Africa, the possibility of outlasting them was born. Ungulates of the African savannah and feline carnivores do not have this ability to breath and run at the same time and must stop to "catch their breath." They are anaerobic sprinters. This makes the antelope vulnerable to the longer-lasting and well-organized human group and puts the big cat at a disadvantage to his human counterpart. Like the wolves and hyenas of today, hunting in packs and with communication between members, and adding the efficient grasping hand free to throw or thrust, an efficient hunting ape was developing. These developments were occurring, hand in hand, with supporting developments in man's evolving brain to facilitate the new skills. Man was becoming the ultimate hunter.

These new, long distance runners, explained the nakedness of the ape-man. Running long distances on the African veldt must have been a hot job. If one is to run long distances, one has to develop a cooling mechanism. Their hair became a detriment and so was "lost", except for that specialized for decoration and perhaps camouflage of the genitals. Later as they moved north and experienced the ice ages, they were already skilled in securing animal hides for warmth, so the body hair was not needed.

As Morris saw it, this was a hunting group of males. The females were too busy rearing and bearing children to play a major role in chasing down and catching prey. Even in a nomadic lifestyle, there was a place where the women and children gathered while the men were out hunting. For many groups, this developed into a more permanent "home base" or series of "home bases" as they followed game migrations. Hunting groups could make longer and more wide-spread forays for meat, while camping next to what little edible vegetation they could find. Women became the repositories of plant identification and use for edible and medicinal purposes. As knowledge grew of migration patterns and useful vegetation, "home bases" became favored. The hunting ape became a territorial ape. Territoriality meant disputes among groups – wars if you will. Another characteristic of man was born.

If we accept the history of our evolution as it has been meticulously discovered by our anthropologist brothers and sisters, and as outlined above, we see that at least the males of the species arose essentially as primate predators.

So, we now have all the elements of what make the modern human. For millions of years the males formed hunting groups, the women stayed together supporting one another. A division of labor developed based on the biological realities and importance of children to the survival of the tribe. The women stayed around an assigned area that was useful for gathering and their children's protection, to be joined later by the men as the light gave out and danger increased. Men became territorial, fighting with other groups over choice locations and access to females. Females worked together closely and were highly motivated to support one another as pregnancy and infant care rotated among them. Support in childbirth was essential to survival. The social glue that held them together was evolving right along with their expanding brains.

We are, no doubt, still evolving, but trappings of modern man have only existed for perhaps forty thousand years - not nearly enough time in evolutionary terms, to have significantly changed the characteristics that were so useful to our ancestor's survival for millions. We still possess the caveman brain and body.

As this model evolved, its success had other repercussions. As the new hominids brain grew, its full growth could not be accommodated in any reasonable gestation period. The monkey brain has attained 70% of its adult size by birth and attains the other 30% in the first six months of life. In our own species, the brain at birth is only twenty-three percent of its final adult size. More importantly, it takes six years to obtain the majority of further growth and the process is not completed until about the twenty-third year of life! This much longer period of dependence was supported by, and further drove development of the "home-base" territoriality of the new species. In order to compete and survive, our best tool was our brain. In order to have a brain that sophisticated, it takes a long time of protecting and nurturing the young. The culture of modern man was solidified.

Unfortunately, sexual maturity does not always correlate with brain development. Brain maturity does not occur until ten years after sexual maturity in Homo sapiens as opposed to six years before sexual maturity in the chimpanzee. This makes for a dangerous mismatch in humans that requires cultural surveillance and control. While the females were being increasingly confined to home base by the dependence of the young, a bunch of adolescent males really interested in sex would pose a problem. The mature males would be useful in managing this issue, if they took some natural interest in the discipline of the developing adolescent boys. As they became sexually mature, these boys would also become useful in the hunt, thereby providing a natural mentoring paradigm. They could be withdrawn from the females for a good part of the day and brought into a hierarchy with the men that would provide the necessary control and structure to channel their newborn sexual interest. Even after the men returned, the boys still existed under the watchful eye of the dominant males.

Lastly, a final problem needed to be overcome as man became a successful hunter. Virile males going off on long trips of any kind is essentially unheard of in other primates. This would leave the females and children unprotected and would invite sexual advances from neighboring tribes. A new adaptation was necessary – pair-bonding. This development of relationships between individual males and females, while not always secure, allowed for the possibility of longer and wider hunts. It also was a key adaptation in supporting the prolonged dependence of the young, in that, a female could rely on protein being brought back specifically to her and her children in exchange for exclusive sexual access. Humans were becoming more modern. The naked ape developed the capacity to fall in love and become sexually imprinted (at least for long enough to support dependent offspring) on a single partner.

Here the new adaptive behavior has to overcome the earlier pattern of promiscuity in primates. Perhaps too commonly, males (and females) still fall back into earlier primate behavior at the earliest dissatisfaction or frustration with their mate. However, this all too frequent event of sex among humans outside our primary relationship does not negate the dominance of pair-bonding in our species. Indeed, evolutionary attempts to secure pair-bonding in early man explains human sexual response. In other primates, the female is only receptive around the time of ovulation, that period when she is most likely to become pregnant. Dramatic physical signals accompany this time, swelling and bright coloration of the genitals for example, alerting the males to her availability. Actual sexual intercourse only lasts a few seconds and no pleasure is apparent in either party. Coupling may occur with several males or the same dominant male several times with a single female at the height of her cycle.

Humans needed something that would support pair-bonding. Evolution supplied it. The female cycle became hidden, without obvious physical changes in the female body to signal every male around. The human vagina evolved to a more downward angle, more comfortably accommodating face to face intercourse and creating stimulation of the clitoris by the male pelvic bone. Females became receptive all through their cycle and even during pregnancy. The male needn't look elsewhere if she presented herself persuasively or was at least willing, when he returned to drop the meat on the fire. Sexual intercourse became more of a private affair, as opposed to out in the open in front of other adults and children. Such adaptations in female human sexual response supported the pair-bonding so important to her welfare, her children's welfare and through them, tribal and species welfare.

CHAPTER TWO:
ELAINE MORGAN

It is important that we establish a shared foundation of knowledge of the consensus regarding the nature of man, accepted by anthropologists, before we launch into modern scholarship on the gender differences in the human brain and their implications. We need to understand where we were for millions of years - where we came from – in order to understand these underlying gender brain differences that supported this way of being that existed until very recently. However, before we go on, this background foundation would not be complete without a thorough review of *The Descent of Woman* by Elaine Morgan (1972). In her feminist rebuttal to Desmond Morris, she appropriately points out that all natural selection in the species did not occur because males were changing and females were reacting to these changes. It is much more likely that the female of the species adaptations were being initiated with equal frequency and being reacted to by the male. In fact, in order to fully appreciate the differences in the male and female brain one has to imagine them co-evolving. They were and still are complementing one another in a give-and-take success strategy.

In the primate species from which we evolved, generally males are bigger than females. This, along with the relative inconvenience of hunting while significantly pregnant, set up the males to become the main hunters. They were bigger and stronger even before the new ape/hominid began to adapt toward upright hunting mode. In addition, because of the social nature of the species and the promiscuity natural to these same early primates, competition between males for access to females was intense. Nature provided testosterone making the male of the species much more aggressive, giving each male a chance to sow his seed, but making the strongest, the most aggressive and the dominant, father of most of the children. Nature assumes that the "best" ape has the best DNA. We are all familiar with gorilla and other great ape hierarchies. The "silver back" rules the roost until he is overthrown by a younger male. Again, this aggressive characteristic of our ancestral primates facilitated the males becoming the hunters. Aggression, adrenaline, rage: useful in open combat or killing other species for food. It is not pretty but it's true. We inherited it from the sexual competition of our progenitors. When we had to learn to hunt to survive, the males were better suited to take the primary role. Society didn't develop as "paternalistic" because men plotted it that way. Men became dominant in most societies because of our biological origins. The culture followed.

However, this does not in any way denigrate the female contribution. As necessary as protein and fat was to survival, the supplementation of the diet by gathering can not be undervalued. As any nutritionist knows, all the vitamins and minerals we need cannot be supplied by animals. An entire counter-culture developed around the safety and edibility of plants and their medicinal purposes as well. This was passed through the maternal line.

If anything, of course, the females provide the most important role in any species society – that of carrying the fetus successfully and caring for the children during their prolonged dependency. In this sense, it was a popular overreaction in the 1970's to see men as an accoutrement - a necessary one, but one none the less. ("Women need men like a fish needs a bicycle" was a popular bumper sticker.) Men, however, had developed a useful contribution by becoming the hunters and protectors of the tribe, compared to our tree-dwelling ancestors who could each, male and female, provide for themselves. Again, this new species co-evolved to their *mutual* benefit. As the brain became larger, the head became bigger. As the head became bigger, childbirth became more difficult. As childbirth became more difficult, support of the process became necessary. Other women were necessary to help. Cooperation became more important for the survival of the group. This spawned the development of communication – language. Women were dependent on each other for survival. Grudges and disputes needed to be smoothed over if one was going to get the help one may need to live a peaceful existence, care for the children and assist in childbirth. Even today, women are all about exchanging information and the subtle, skilled soothing of disputes. Men are all about linear thinking with blinders on to emotional content – theirs and others. The latter facilitates hunting. The former facilitates group cooperation and mutual support. Men tend to be mutually supportive in a functional way. Women tend to value the cultivation of good feelings among themselves (as we will see in the subsequent chapter on modern brain research) as an investment in their future. They will need those other women. Relatively few men can, in a pinch, impregnate many women, so why not let the men take the high risk behavior. It only makes sense if the success of the tribe depends on offspring.

But don't be fooled. We need each other. Any species that evolved supporting brain function for the long periods of time the men worked together and supporting brain structures for the long periods of time the women were together, no doubt developed, with the same diligence, the supporting thoughts and feelings that facilitated our time together as well. Women facilitate social organization and functioning because it is their nature. Their emotional competence is the glue that holds a tribe together. Men may love their shared time together, but sooner rather than later, come back to home base to be reassured by the familiar efficiency of home base.

Finally, we have to review our previous comments on human sexual response, derived from Desmond Morris, from a woman's point of view. Compared to earlier primates, what incentive did hominid females have to make themselves available to a male anytime, anywhere? To encourage them to bring home the bacon? Sure. To ensure protection for their children? Absolutely! But nature provided a much more powerful stimulus. Women began to enjoy sex. Remember that in monkeys intercourse lasts a few seconds. Neither gender shows signs of enjoyment. The female's receptivity is driven by the cycle of her hormones. This is the same essential cycle in the human female. What changed? Sex between the new naked apes must have become more and more enjoyable for the female. It lasted longer, was focused on a single male mate who she came to appreciate as a partner, and resulted in orgasm in the female as well as the male. Unheard of! Women having orgasms! It would be enough to encourage them to seek out their mate on a regular basis, probably every night after supper. Evolution provided a reward for women that cemented the pair-mating bond that was so important for the species after such prolonged dependency of children had developed. Evolution of women's sexual response may be the single most important adaptation supporting our new species survival. Instead of one female coming into estrus at a time (or more likely nearly all at once) and the males fighting over them, causing grievous bodily harm, women developed a mechanism that made each guy feel special and decreased the consequences of fighting at the same time. Men all had something to look forward to when they got home. "Let's knock off early – what do you say?", "Hey, great idea!" More and more we recognize the origin of modern human relations.

Hairless Revisited

As an aside, Ms. Morgan emphasizes a different reason for the nakedness of the "naked ape": It is quite plausible. Say that when our ancestors starting testing terrestrial living, they would at first be poorly prepared and would be easy prey for the awesome predators of the time. They would never have the opportunity to evolve into the hunters that allowed survival. Sir Alister Hardy had previously developed an "aquatic ape" hypothesis and it was duly mentioned in passing by Desmond Morris. Morgan brings it to popular awareness in her book.

It seems that one of the advantages of being an ape was that one could stand upright. It was an awkward but common practice. Say one of the early experiments with terrestrial apes occurred near a body of water. When threatened by predators, the apes walked into the water deeper than their four-legged pursuers. The water provided protection. Seem far-fetched?

Consider the evidence. Hair is a disadvantage in the water and would eventually be lost. The residual hair pattern, seen most clearly on the human newborn, before it is lost, is arranged in a perfect hydrodynamic pattern, as if swimming. Humans have a subcutaneous layer of fat. This is something found only in ocean going mammals and foreign to terrestrial ones. It keeps one warm in the water. Good for the northern latitudes and ice ages, which explains our ability to move from Africa to Northern Europe in a relatively short period of time (less than a hundred thousand years).

It is not an accident that human remains are found most commonly along bodies of water as the new hominid worked his way up rivers from the ocean. Large bodies of water would have provided the kind of small biological diversity that a new non-tree going primate would have needed. Apes were used to supplementing their diet with small game common to trees and in the water ample crustaceans would be available without being fleet of foot and bird eggs would be plentiful on the shoreline. Early tools to crush the shells would be instantly available. It is not surprising then that the early migration of early man out of Africa followed patterns along the coastlines at first, then went inland. What about the caveman? Where are the caves on the African savannah? Oh, but there are plenty along the coast line where water forms them naturally. So, a lucky monkey, searching the ground for food, senses a stalking predator, and panic-stricken, retreats into the ocean with nothing but his head sticking out. Eventually, the big cat gets tired of waiting. This monkey must have spent a lot of time in the water those early millions of years. It turns out that all water favoring mammals are hairless – seals, dolphins, whales, hippos, elephants, pigs, etc. (The elephant's closest relative is the elephant seal.) If only one's head sticks out of the water, why have hair anywhere else? They either stayed permanently in the water or kept it as part of their natural habitat, as pigs, elephants, hippos and rhinos do to cool off. Having spent all this time in the water, early man became better and better at standing up – better and better at walking – with longer and longer legs and a different spine to pelvis axis, just as previously hypothesized for running with a spear. Except it developed in the water first, then was used for hunting on land. Early tool-making and use had already developed to open the shells. Early man just came on shore and hit bigger things with his rock. As he got to be a more formidable hunter his forays inland could be longer and wider. All the rest of the history follows. Home base became the cave on the coastline.

The final clincher to this theory's attraction is the dive reflex. When whales, dolphins or seals dive, their hearts slow down to enable a longer, deeper dive. Of terrestrial animals, only one species has a dive reflex – man. Try it sometime. Try splashing cold water on your face. A sudden deep reflexive breath and a suppressed heart rate ensues. Explain that, Desmond.

However, as brilliant as Morgan has been in delineating a more equal appreciation of the evolution of the human species, she does not deny this basic truth - humans developed as a hunter-gatherer, communal, territorial species. This way of living existed simultaneously with the development of the modern brain. Hence, the pathways and functionalities were designed to facilitate this paradigm of survival. "The watershed for (the female hominid) was the hunting-gathering era, which established the division of labor and the nuclear family." (*The Descent of Woman*, pg. 208) This underlies all we will come to know about why our brains are the way they are today.

CHAPTER THREE:
THE MALE VERSUS THE FEMALE BRAIN

"You Mean He's HARDWIRED That Way?"
One of These Things is NOT Like the Other

"They are the same only in their common membership in the same species. To maintain that they are the same in aptitude, skill or behavior is to build a society based on a biological and scientific lie. The sexes are different because their brains are different. The brain, the chief administrative and emotional organ of life, is differently constructed in men and in women; it processes information in a different way, which results in different perceptions, priorities and behavior. In the past ten years there has been an explosion of scientific research into what makes the sexes different. Doctors, scientists, psychologists and sociologists, working apart, have produced a body of findings which, taken together, paints a remarkably consistent picture. And the picture is one of startling sexual asymmetry." (*Brain Sex*, pg.5).

A RECKONING

Let's start with the facts. From early in uterine life, men's and women's brains are different. The scientific awareness first arose with I.Q. tests in the 1960's. Researchers noticed consistent differences favoring one sex over the other in some of the abilities tested. Dr. Wechsler, the father of the modern I.Q. test, considered these differences a nuisance and tried to eliminate all those areas that resulted in significant gender differences. Finding this impossible, he and others developed male-slanted and female-slanted tests to approximate equal average scores. Even so, gender differences continued to emerge. For example, out of one hundred-five tests measuring skills in solving maze puzzles, involving the most heterogeneous populations throughout the world, including from most primitive to highly civilized societies, ninety-nine percent showed an undeniable superiority for males in this ability. Almost in exasperation, Wechsler stated, "…men not only behave but 'think' differently from women." This statement did not reach public knowledge. Attempts ensued among professionals to sociologically explain these data away for many years into the future. It turns out Wechsler was right. The genders are different because their brains are different. The brain, the chief administrative and emotional organ of life, as stated above, is differently constructed in men and women. It is designed to facilitate different primary purposes. It processes information in a different way, which results in different perceptions, priorities and behaviors.

"Infants are not blank slates, on whom we scrawl instructions for sexually appropriate behavior. They are born with male or female minds of their own. They have, quite literally, made up their minds in the womb, safe from the legions of social engineers that impatiently await them." (*Brain Sex*, pg. 20)

If there is still a dispute about how sex differences arise, there is now no argument in the scientific community that such differences exist. It cannot be stressed enough however that this book concerns itself with the average man and the average woman. In the same way, we might say that men are taller than women. Look across any crowded room and this will be obvious. Of course some women will be taller than some men, and the tallest woman may possibly be taller than the tallest man. But statistically men are on average seven per cent taller, and the tallest person in the world, rather than in the room, is most certainly a man.

The statistical variations in sex differences which we will explore, in skill, aptitudes or abilities, are much greater than they are in relation to height. However, there will always be the exception to the average. The exception does not invalidate the general, average rule.

THE SENSES

At a few hours old, girls are more sensitive than boys to touch. Tests between the sexes of tactile sensitivity in the hands and fingers produce differences so striking that sometimes female and male scores do not even overlap. This persists into adulthood as women react more acutely to pain but contrasts with the finding that men have a higher threshold and tolerance for sudden physical pain, while women have a higher resistance to long-term discomfort. This is an evolutionary difference that prepares males and females for the roles they had for millions of years before the current era (roughly the last hundred thousand years). Men needed to be less sensitive to pain, both in their peripheral nerves and in their brain perception, in their primary role as hunters. Women needed to be more sensitive to touch for their role in the subtleties of gathering and child care. In a sample of young adults, females showed "overwhelmingly" greater sensitivity to pressure on the skin on every part of the body. In childhood and persisting into maturity, women have a tactile sensitivity so superior to men's that there is no overlap between the scores of the two sexes. The least sensitive women are more sensitive than the most sensitive man, identical to that of female vs. male babies at a few days old. It is not meant to imply by stating this that men and women are "locked into" these old roles. Rather, it explains how vastly different men and women *are* as a result of this evolution. Much of the criticism of men is based on the denial of the reality of these differences.

When it comes to sound, infant females are much less tolerant. One researcher believes that they "hear" noises as being twice as loud as do males (hence the reference to "that tone of voice"). Baby girls become irritated and anxious about noise, pain or discomfort more readily than baby boys. Infant girls will turn in response to sounds to which male babies don't respond.

Baby girls are more easily comforted by soothing words and singing. Six times as many girls as boys can sing in tune. Even before they can understand language, girls seem to be better than boys at identifying the emotional content of speech. From the outset of life, girl babies show a greater degree of interest in communicating with other people. One study involves babies of only 2-4 days old. It shows that girls attend almost twice as long, maintaining eye contact with a silent adult, and girls also look longer than boys when the adult is talking. Boys are just as happy with an object dangling in front of them as a person standing there. Not so for girls. The boy's attention span was the same, whether the adult was talking to them or not – showing a bias toward what they could see rather than what they could hear. The male brain is designed to focus on what he can see – a hunter's style, if you will.

From the cradle, baby girls like to gurgle at humans. Females are meant to value communication. Most boys are just as talkative, but are equally happy to jabber away at cot toys or looking at abstract geometric designs. These differences are apparent in the very first hours after birth. The different bias toward the personal shows itself in other ways. At four months, most baby girls can distinguish photographs of people they know from photographs of strangers. Boys cannot.

Men see better in bright light. Women see better in the dark. Men see in a more narrow field, like a race horse with mild blinders on, focusing on the track ahead. Men see more depth with better perspective. Women see a wider field of vision, literally taking in the big picture. This is determined by the mixture and placement of the receptor rods and cones in the back of the eye. Women have a better visual memory. Women's sense of smell and taste are more acute than men – up to six times better in most studies. All these differences, these adaptations are not random and explain the difficulties of gender communication.

ACTION

Boy babies are more active and wakeful than girls. It is the male wired brain of activity-seeking at work. Action is preferred over people. As months go by and the child stands upright, the boys tend to show a greater interest than girls in exploring the corners of their small world. Their greater muscle mass is already evident and facilitates this, allowing them to range farther than their sisters. They make fewer journeys back to the reassuring base camp of mother. Scientists have devised a test where a barrier is strung across the playroom, separating mother and child. The girls tended to stand at the center of the barrier and cry; the boys made little safaris to the edge of the obstacle to see if there was a way around it.

PLAY

The sexes differ in the way they play. According to one English study, having said goodbye to their mothers at the school gates (taking an average of 92.5 seconds for girls, 36 seconds for boys), boys will wheel off into the playground. There, they will play more vigorously, and occupy a much larger playing space than the girls. In the playschool classroom, the boys will be much more interested in building structures out of blocks, playing with any kind of vehicle – indeed with anything which does something – be it a door handle, or an electric switch.

Girls opt for more sedentary games, and, if they build will tend to build long, low structures while boys go for toppling height in their creations. Again, boys are designed to be out and physically active to best serve the species. Girls are designed to be more content, preferring more to stay in a more communal setting where conversation is the most important part of life.

A newcomer to the play group – of either sex – will tend to be greeted with friendship and curiosity by the girls; with indifference by the boys. There is irritation if the newcomer follows the boys about. Girls will tend to welcome the stranger into their group. Boys and girls have different styles foreshadowing the future for boys in competition and for women in mutual support. Not very effective for men in communicating with women but that's just the point. Communicating with women was not a high priority on the survival metrics for men as hunters.

By the age of four, boys and girls usually play apart, having instituted their own form of infant sexual segregation. Boys tend not to bother about whether or not they like any particular member of the gang. He is included if he is useful. Girls exclude other girls if "they're not nice." Girls accept younger children into the group. Boys tend to try to join groups of older children. Girls know and remember the names of their playmates. Boys often don't. Boys will make up stories of zap, POW and villainy. Girl's narratives focus on home, friendship, emotions. Boys will tell the story of the robber. Girls tell the same tale from the point of view of the victim. Again, this is not cultural training. It is not how we are raised. It is who we are. One prominent woman anthropology researcher exclaimed: "After fifteen years looking for an environmental explanation (for male/female differences) and getting zero results, I gave up." (Camilla Benbow) The next step in our

17

evolution as a species is to first accept who we are, then and only then can we make decisions about how to move on.

SEX

You might say, "What about sex?" Of course, that was important but the most attractive female partners tended to be chosen by a dominance competition among men. For women, attractiveness as a provider was the dominant criteria for choosing mates. Again, two different criteria for partner selection are used by males and females. This is still true today, whether we like to admit it or not. Women choose men in every modern study by their intelligence and verbal skills, sense of humor and physical appearance, especially broad shoulders and height. These are characteristics that correlate with better providership; higher salaries, better genes for the kids, and the hope of a better success for a woman's offspring. Picking attractive mates from a point of view of the health and safety of one's progeny is still the case, whether women intend to have children or not. It's in their genes. "Power is a strong aphrodisiac." (Nancy Kissinger)

Men have been found to pick women most strongly, not by beauty of their face or how big their breasts are (a common misconception) but by their waist to hip ratio – a surrogate for fecundity.

SPATIAL ABILITY

The area of the biggest differences, and most consistent, have been documented in what scientists call "spatial ability." This is the ability to picture and manipulate objects in three-dimensional space, their shape, position, geography and proportion, accurately in the mind's eye. A quarter of women perform a task assembling a three dimensional apparatus better than the average male. At the top end of this scale of mechanical aptitude there will be twice as many men as women. Three-dimensional construction, map and blueprint reading and abstract mathematical and chess skills are included in this aptitude. Women can even up their map-reading scores by simply turning the map around. Males of any mammalian species tested are much better at negotiating and learning mazes then females. This apparently correlates with three-dimensional spatial ability. Women can find their way much faster if landmarks are included. They have excellent memory for landmarks and apparently find their way in space in this way – best suited for moving from one known area to another rather than in an unknown space. Chess, of course, has been traditionally dominated by men, even in a country like Russia where it is a game enjoyed by all.

From school age onwards, boys will generally outperform girls in areas of mathematics involving abstract concepts of space, relationships, and theory. At the very highest level of mathematical excellence, according to the biggest survey ever conducted, the very best boys totally eclipse the very best girls. Drs. Camilla Benbow and Julian Stanley, working with highly gifted students of both sexes, found that the very best girl never beat the very best boy. Furthermore, they discovered a startling sex ratio of mathematical brilliance: for every exceptional girl there were more than thirteen exceptional boys. In young adolescent children, it was found that boys often use "unknown variables" in their minds to solve problems even though they have not yet been introduced to algebra. Girls rarely do. Isaac Newton invented calculus in order to leap to the intuitive conclusions in his laws of motion, but then rewrote the proof in Euclidian geometry *Philosophiæ Naturalis Principia Mathematica* (1687), in order for it to be understood and accepted at the time. Einstein's "thought experiments" were the basis of all his original work, which was written out belatedly and anticlimactically for him. Stephen Hawking is a modern day man who entertains incredibly complex concepts and ideas and follows them to a conclusion in his mind alone.

These differences in spatial ability support a marked difference in testing men's and women's ability to judge the relative distance travelled by two objects and the velocity of two moving objects relative to one another. Men are more accurate at judging the arrival time of such objects (judging when an object moving toward them would either impact them or pass them) by sight or even hearing.

Boys on average have superior eye-hand coordination. This is not a result of practice but presents itself as early as two years of age, where boys are significantly more able to throw, kick or hit a ball. On the other hand, girls show a greater fine motor control, hand-eye coordination, manipulating small objects.

VERBAL ABILITY–COMMUNICATION SKILLS

Here the female brain leads the male brain from as early as it can be measured. Girls and women do better on tests of verbal ability from the earliest testing. Girls say their first words and learn to speak in short sentences earlier than boys. They read better too. At the age of three, 99% of speech of girls is comprehensible. It takes boys a year longer. It took Einstein five years to speak. Girls grasp the early rudiments of grammar, punctuation and spelling better on average. Girls and women outperform boys and men on measures of general reading ability in elementary school, middle school, high school, and in the general population of adults. This can be understood as being related to their advantage in language competencies. Three out of four women commit fewer speech errors (i.e., retrieving the wrong word). Nine out of ten women outperformed the average man in the ability to discriminate among basic language sounds. Nearly nine out of ten men had more frequent pauses in their utterances that the average woman. These findings represent some of the largest cognitive sex differences ever documented, very near the differences in spatial ability/math testing. Boys out-number girls 4:1 in remedial reading classes. Stuttering occurs almost exclusively in males. Girls and women find it easier to acquire foreign languages skills. Math score tend to even up if the questions are posed as word problems.

Across all samples, girls and women showed an advantage over boys and men for accuracy in judging emotional cues on the bases of facial expressions, body posture, and vocal intonation. The advantage of girls and women was found in the same general magnitude in all nations tested. When non-verbal cues are assessed, 17 out of 20 girls and women were more accurate at decoding the emotional cues of another individual than the average same age boy or man. Also, 17 out of 20 women are judged to convey more information in their facial expressions than the average man. Men in prehistoric times often took females from outside their immediate families and brought them into their group. This meant that men had a close-knit kinship with their hunting group, which was often, quite literally, their brothers, cousins, parents and children, while women had to scramble to make friends quickly and effectively with a group of women they had never seen before. Preparation for this process starts in the womb, in the first few days of life, and is evident at birth. A group of children given a special sort of sight test, looked through a contraption like a pair of binoculars, which showed the left and right eye two different images at the same time. Through one side was an object. Through the other was a person. They varied from eye to eye. When asked what they had seen, boys reported seeing significantly more things than people. Girls reported more people than things. As we can see, males and females brains are built with different primary skills.

An explosion of human evolution took place starting a hundred thousand years ago. The human brain reached its current form. Coincident with this time we see the rise of modern civilization: sophisticated tools, agriculture, art and music, self-decoration, philosophy and spirituality. The greatest areas of expansion of the human brain that had most recently occurred to facilitate this, was in areas associated with language. It was the development of language that spawned this great cultural leap forward. Much of the confusion and conflict in the American gender war is due to a failure to understand that the languages used by men and women tend to be sex specific. Over the vast reaches of time before this development of language, our ancestors lived in small tribes where men were primarily warriors and hunters and women were primarily gatherers. Since the terms of survival for male hunters and female gatherers were quite different, natural selection favored the evolution of disparate emotional and cognitive processes in the brains of men and women. This different way of processing and valuing information and emotions was already set up when language came on board as a new skill. On measurements of various aptitude tests, the differences between the sexes in average scores on these tests can be as much as 25%. A difference of as little as five per cent has been found to have a marked impact on men's and women's activities or occupations. This is not meant to exclude girls or boys from occupational or societal opportunities. It is simply an explanation of the remedial reading and "math phobia" that we want to explain away culturally, for example. What science has to say about the alternative ways in which information is processed in the brain is fascinating and allows us to understand why the communication styles, interests, and expectations of men and women tend to diverge.

While men use conversation to "preserve their independence and negotiate and maintain status in a hierarchical social order," women use conversation as "a way of establishing connections and negotiating relationships." (Deborah Tannen, *You Just Don't Understand: Women and Men in Conversation*).

ANATOMICAL CORRELATION

The human brain is an archeological site with the deepest levels consisting of the most ancient structures and the outer layers of the more recently evolved areas. Our shared evolutionary history with the reptiles is the brain region that sits above the spinal chord. It consists of the medulla, the cerebellum and the pons. These areas control breathing, heart rate, digestion, coordination of muscle movement and relays for breathing, hearing, feeding and facial expression.

The next most recently evolved area, essentially alike in all mammals, is the source of emotions. The limbic system sits above the brain stem and is interconnected from below and to above, linking thoughts to feelings and involuntary reactions. The thalamus dominates the region and directs all information from the senses to the cortex. It is not surprising that the massa intermedia, a band of tissue that connects the right and left halves of the thalamus, and therefore links the left and right halves of the brain, has been found to be significantly larger in women than in men. Although male brains are typically more massive than those of females (related to overall size of the animal), the massa intermedia is 53 percent bigger in females. The linkage between sensory input, thoughts and emotions, as we have seen, is much more facile in women than in men. The amygdala is part of the limbic system and triggers aggressive behaviors, fearful reactions and positive associations. The hypothalamus controls the endocrine glands, key players as the brain differentiates.

Finally we have the neocortex – the overlying outer region of the brain, most recently evolved. The occipital lobes, located in the back of the head, are the primary visual areas. The temporal lobes, positioned above the ears, are intimately connected with the limbic system below and the sensory input, both auditory and visual. The overarching areas in the center of the brain, the parietal lobes, are a schematic map of the motor and tactile responses of the brain. The two frontal lobes are control centers that "decide" consciously which responses to make based on input from the other regions of the brain. This region has undergone most recent evolutionary expansion. It is what gives us choice.

In people with typical hemispheric dominance, the left side manages linguistic analysis and expression. The right hemisphere is responsible for perception of spatial relationships, faces, emotional stimuli, and the meaning of vocal intonations that modify the literal meaning of a word. Again, the area connecting the two hemispheres in these higher brain functions, the corpus callosum, is nearly fifty percent bigger in the female brain.

Gender differences in these regions are quite prominent. Hundreds of studies on brain-damaged individuals have shown that cognitive tasks are more widely distributed throughout both hemispheres in female brains. Based on recent PET technology studies, it has been revealed that cognitive tasks in the female brain tend to be spread over both hemispheres, and the same tasks in the male brain tend to be localized in one hemisphere. (see *Left Brain, Right Brain*, Springer and Deutsch.) This means that the male and female pattern of brain organization has advantages and disadvantages for both sexes. The tighter organization and localized function of the male brain are suited for coherence, linearity and quick action/reaction. While functional language is important for men, it is not as valued, as measured by the duplication of the female brain to support it, and it is not nearly as well linked to associated emotional content. The key word here is functional. That's what language is to the average male. For women and girls, communication is the backbone of existence, as opposed to action for the male. Language skills are protected and purposefully linked to emotional meanings. Men suffering a stroke to their left hemisphere, involving the speech area, are much more often permanently impaired in their understanding and speaking then women, who have a similar backup area on the right side, and soon recover function, even if the left is their dominant side.

Functional MRI scanning has extended these studies. In a Yale University School of Medicine study, thirty-eight right-handed subjects, nineteen males and nineteen females, were shown visual questions. The results showed that the male brain performs these tasks in an area known as the inferior frontal gyrus of the dominant hemisphere only and that the female brain performs these tasks in the inferior frontal gyrus of both hemispheres. Another study, combining PET and functional MRI to image the metabolic status of the brain regions, found seventeen regions of the brain in which there were sex differences.

Significantly, men, on average, have more activity in the temporal limbic system, a primitive brain region associated with action, while women, on average, have more activity in the middle and posterior cingulated gyrus, a more recently evolved area associated with symbolic action. One author explained the distinction as follows: "If a dog is angry and bites, that's an action. If he is angry and bares his fangs and growls, that is a symbolic action."

More interaction with the right hemisphere in female brains, would enhance the range and complexity of linguistic representations. Women are more skilled in small, precise eye-hand coordination and precise hand movements. The area associated with hand movements is closely associated with the anterior portion of the left hemisphere, where linguistic functions in female brains are more concentrated. Women were "gathering" as they developed and improved their language skills it seems. Therefore their fine new language skills are forever linked to their fine motor skills. The posterior portion of the brain, where linguistic functions in males are more densely clustered, lies closer in proximity to both the visual cortex and the brain regions that coordinate limb and muscle movements. It seems the male brain linked the new language skills with hunting.

More global differences in cognitive and emotional styles can also be attributed to the sex-specific human brain. The superior linguistic abilities of women, particularly associational fluency, coupled with more symmetry in hemispheric functions, could explain why women tend to be better intuitional thinkers in the personal realm. If linguistically constructed reality in the brains of women is more richly configured and interconnected, it should follow that women on average are more attuned to nuances, hidden meanings and their associations than men. Men are more intuitive in the spatial-abstract, non-verbal realm. In the male brain, the more independent functioning of the left hemisphere probably makes linguistic constructions of reality more factual, linear and goal-directed, since the left brain is the "executive" center of the brain. Less feedback from the right hemisphere may contribute to reduced awareness of coded meanings in relationships, emotional stimuli and vocal intonations.

A conversation from Anne Tyler's novel, *The Accidental Tourist*, is illustrative. The conversation begins when Macon makes an observation about Muriel's son.

Macon: *"I don't think Alexander's getting a proper education,"* he said to her one evening.

Muriel: *"Oh, he's okay."*

Macon: *"I asked him to figure what change they'd give back when we bought the milk today, and he didn't have the faintest idea. He didn't even know he'd have to subtract."*

Muriel: *"Well, he's only in second grade."*

Macon: *"I think he ought to go to private school."*

Muriel*: "Private schools cost money."*

Macon*: "So? I'll pay."*

She stopped flipping the bacon and looked over at him.

"What are you saying?" she said.

Macon: *"Pardon."*

Muriel: *"What are you saying, Macon? Are you saying you're committed?"*

Muriel then tells Macon that he must decide whether he wants to divorce his wife and marry her. She will not put her son in a new school when he could be forced to leave if Macon returns to his wife. Macon is mystified by her leap to implication.

Macon: *"But I just want him to learn to subtract."*

The problem is that Macon is concerned with the message, the simple matter of Alexanders's learning math. But Muriel is concerned with the much larger implication. What would it say about the *relationship* if he began paying for her son's education?

CHAPTER FOUR:

HORMONES

What makes male and female brains different? Now that we understand why we evolved in a complementary but different way, let's explore the how.

We all share the same sexual identity for only the first few weeks after conception. Thereafter, in the womb, the very structure and pattern of the brain begins to take specifically male or female form. Hormones determine the distinct male or female organization of the brain as it develops in the womb. The influence of sex hormones on brain cells creates a "set" that is highly resistant to change after birth. Each sex has a mind of its own at birth. Throughout infant, teenage, and adult life, the way the brain was forged will have a subtle interplay with the hormones, and a fundamental effect on the attitudes, behavior, and intellectual and emotional functioning of the individual. Innate differences in brain structure mean that from infancy and through childhood, the male and female paths increasingly diverge. Biology, accentuated by social attitudes, which may themselves have a biological base, gives men and women different priorities, ambitions and behavior. As American neurologist Dr. Richard Restak asserts: "It seems unrealistic to deny any longer the existence of male and female brain differences. Just as there are physical dissimilarities between male and female ... there are equally dramatic differences in brain functioning." The way our brains are made affects how we think, see, feel, smell, communicate, love, make love, fight, succeed or fail. Understanding how our brains and those of the opposite gender work is a matter of no little importance.

In the first few weeks in the womb, the tiny fetus isn't noticeably a miniature girl or a miniature boy. It has all the basic equipment, such as vestigial ducts, tracts and so on, to develop as either sex. As the weeks go by, however, the genes begin to put the message across. If things go normally for a boy, and follow the XY blueprint, the chromosomes will cue the development of the gonads into testes. It's now, at around six weeks, that sexual identity is determined. The male fetus develops the special cells which produce the male hormones or androgens, the main one being testosterone. The hormones instruct the body not to bother with developing a feminine set of sexual equipment, while stimulating the development of embryonic male genitalia.

At about the same time, if the baby is a female, genetically XX, the reproductive machinery develops along female lines, produces no significant amount of male hormone, produces scant female hormones, and results in a baby girl by default. The embryonic brain develops "female" anatomy, physiology and organization.

Just as male gender sexual organs depended on the presence of male hormone, coded by the Y chromosome, to divert the body from developing along a female line, so a radical intervention is needed to change that "default" female brain structure into a male pattern. This literally mind-altering event occurs as embryonic male babies are exposed to a colossal dose of male hormone at the critical time when their brains are beginning to take shape. The male hormone levels around six weeks in the womb, when the testes develop, are four times the level experienced throughout infancy and boyhood. A vast surge of male hormone occurs at each end of the male development: adolescence, when his sexuality comes on stream, and six weeks after conception, at the moment his brain is beginning to take shape. We have all been aware of the former surge, which results in such dramatic physical and behavior changes but up until the last ten years we weren't aware of the initial intrauterine surge making the baby come out "all boy" from the beginning.

Final confirmation of the effects of hormones on the brain comes from research with "abnormal" individuals. Congenital adrenal hyperplasia is a fairly common (1 in 10-18,000 female births) condition that occurs when the adrenal glands produce secretions in the womb that are similar to male hormones. Girls may have normal lives as women, conceiving and bearing children. They have an XX chromosome complement. However, their mothers often say, if the child is identified for some reason (delayed menstruation is common) that they never acted like a typical girl. They play noticeably rougher and tougher. They spend most of their time outdoors and seek out the company of boys preferentially as playmates. They have no time for dolls. In school, they are later in developing reading and writing skills than the average girl but similar to the average boy. Their brains are significantly masculinized by their intrauterine exposure to unusually high male hormones for a female fetus.

Turner syndrome girls (1 in 2000 female births) are born with an XO complement of sex chromosomes. They do not develop ovaries in the womb. Normally a small amount of male hormones are found in the fetal milieu of even girl babies. Turner syndrome girls are not exposed to any male hormone because of the lack of gonads. They universally express an exaggerated femininity. They play with dolls to almost the exclusion of everything else. They are very romantic and dream of getting married and having children – alas, something they cannot do. They love to baby sit. They score the average of girls on tests of verbal ability but far below average girls on tests of spatial ability. They have a chronically terrible sense of direction. If often takes them years to learn their way to school.

Many documented cases now have been followed of male children whose mothers were given supplementary female hormones during pregnancy. They tend to be shy, unassertive and have comparatively low self-esteem. They tend to be poor athletes, are often regarded as a "sissy" by their peers and attempt to avoid rather than confront conflict. Men who are known to have been exposed to a below average amount of male hormone in the womb, are also found to have a female pattern in the distribution of their skill functions in the brain.

Anatomic differences mediated by this huge testosterone surge, differentiates all male brains into more focused, segregated, compartmentalized structures. In all females the laying down of information and the emotional context of an encounter with another human being are linked and spread over both hemispheres of the brain. Not so with men, where it tends to be localized and "niched" with less emotional content but more coherence. Hence, a woman in a room full of people or in an intense conversation may draw out myriads of levels of meaning, while a man may just be able to report the facts. A typical woman notices colors, the fabrics, the furniture, the drapes, the knick-knacks, as well as a rainbow constellation of what's going on with the people in the room. A typical man is much less likely to be able to recall much of any of what the room looked like, who was there, what they were wearing, and may be totally oblivious to the emotional content of what was going on with everybody. It is not a problem for him. Having spent millions of years focused on what was right in front of him; thinking linearly, communicating minimally, acting physically, he is now designed to talk about the weather, geography, and competition, in sports and business. Emotional associations have not been "bred" into him. He is less sensitive to touch and relatively insensitive to pain. He may hate the party unless he can find a few other men he knows and find some easy talk. Interestingly, the conversation may eventually turn to more intimate and emotional topics of concern but only if these other people are or have become part of his inner circle - his "hunting party." Most often this doesn't happen and he has to be dragged to these events (unless it's a business lunch of power-brokering where he may be in his element, depending on where he is on the food chain). Other than the grousing about going to the party in the first place, this difference in female and male brain processing is not a problem until his wife asks him what was going on with everybody with which she did not get a chance to talk in person. "What's going on with Bob?" He replies "Same ol', same ol'." She could see from across the room that Bob was in distress but could never quite get there to explore it and doesn't know him very well. Her husband spent half an hour talking to him but couldn't tell anything was wrong standing right in front of him. Nor did Bob choose to discuss it. What would he and Bob say to each other? Offer a solution perhaps, but since neither one is in touch with their feelings naturally, the husband wouldn't gather much information of interest to his wife. She follows up: "How is he doing, now that he and Sally have separated?" He replies: "They've separated?"

It makes sense that a male's brain, being more tightly organized, somehow is helped with the efficiency of visual and spatial relationships, as well as mathematical reasoning, perhaps by the minutely shorter distances or the coherence of the organization of cells with the same function. A woman's more diffuse network and the accompanying increase in communicating fibers, allows for her superiority in communication with other people by linking up her verbal center with a plethora of other sites in the brain holding related information.

An interesting development in brain research has occurred around this difference. Oxytocin – the hormone that physicians were trained to understand drove uterine contractions during delivery, has been found to be primarily a neurotransmitter, i.e., a brain chemical. It seems that, even more importantly than its role in birth, it drives relational behavior. The hormone was discovered in 1953 and found to drive uterine contractions after cervical dilation. It was found to cause a "let down" of milk in nursing women, in response to nipple stimulation by the infant, to facilitate successful breast feeding. Now it has been found in the brain, stimulating feelings of contentment and calmness, decreasing anxiety and increasing feelings of security around one's mate. It stimulates empathy and generosity. It has a role in social recognition and pair-bonding. It is a hormone, while not unique to women, (it is higher in both genders after orgasm), that most symbolizes the female brain. Most recently it has been found that when a woman feels stressed, and she calls another woman to talk (as opposed to a man), her plasma oxytocin level goes up with the conversation. She becomes calmer and is reassured. Men have no such response. The rise in oxytocin secretion from the hypothalamus region of the brain after orgasm in both genders implies it was designed as a powerful bonding agent. While women experience its bonding effects during conversation with other women, birth and breast-feeding, men have only been found to experience effects in response to orgasm. Our brains are telling us something. They are designed to facilitate us as a gender. "Boys are fancy on the outside, girls are fancy on the inside", doesn't just apply to the genitals. A man's relative paucity of these complicating communicative axons and facilitating chemicals, predisposes him to be more focused, since there is substantially less background noise, while he is figuring out a practical spatial problem. Unfortunately, this does not mean he can communicate the answer well when he arrives at it, or even describe the process.

When we add these anatomic differences to the many functional changes mediated biochemically in the womb – the differences in verbal ability, emotional awareness, sensitivity to sound, touch and pain and the inherent difference in desire to interact with other people (as opposed to objects), all of which are apparent at birth – we get a picture of a species made up of men and women that are well-equipped for doing different things and doing them very well. This does not imply that roles are predetermined. This is hardly true in today's society. It does mean that men and women tend to be attracted to different activities and perform the same activity differently. This is not only okay, it is good, a divine design if you will. The sum is greater than the parts. We are meant to complement one another. The frustration is in not understanding this and at least in the last few decades, expecting men and women to be the same in the name of equality, not realizing it is not something one can "cure" with culture. It is built into our brains.

There is one newly found brain chemical, phenylethylamine, that works the same way on both gendered brain substrates. Phenylethylamine, or PEA, is an endogenous amphetamine. It saturates the brain when we fall in love. It causes feelings of giddiness, optimism, euphoria and boundless energy ("they danced the night away"). PEA highs are associated through a feedback loop from the amygdala in the limbic system. This area links exciting events with emotional content. This means that dangerous situations are linked to sexual attraction and bonding. PEA was found to be much higher in the blood stream after sky-diving, for example. If the participants are interviewed after a sky-diving event by an attractive member of the opposite sex, many more sexual references were prevalent in the language used by the responders, and the males much more often pursued the interviewer for a date than a placebo group that participated in a less exhilarating activity. It may be dangerous to let your daughter go out on a date with a player after a game. He is likely to be much more aggressive.

PEA's evolutionary function is to promote mating and transmission of genes. PEA levels are high in new love relationships in both partners. These enhanced levels can be sustained for up to three years. Long enough to have a child, wean it and raise it to walking. Normally, the brain transitions from the PEA high of a new relationship to a longer-lasting relationship by producing more endorphins (morphine-like brain chemicals) as the PEA slackens. The endorphins induce calm, security and well-being, thereby acting to sustain the relationship. However, in relationship studies in diverse societies, the fourth year of a marriage is generally when the peak incidence of divorce occurs, reflecting an unsuccessful transition after the PEA high wears off.

ADOLESCENCE

While the sex of the brain is determined at the time of neural organization in the womb, the difference in brain sex does not show fully until the hormones of puberty come on line. At that point, the ebb and flow of hormones activates and accentuates brain differences. Amazingly, males and females diverge further after puberty! We already know how important the hormones are in organizing the brain by being present at the right time and place and in the right amount. At puberty, the sex hormones complete their role. Not only do they make the sexes behave differently, in terms of aggression or emotionality, they also make the sexes better and worse at different tasks, for each sex has different brain strengths and strategies.

Come puberty, the boys academic skills accelerate dramatically. They catch up with the girls on the verbal and writing scores, ands surge ahead in mathematical ability. Male IQ scores soar between the ages of fourteen and sixteen, while girl's scores tend to level off. On the math part of the SAT, at scores greater than 420 (out of a possible 800), boys outnumber girls 1.5 to 1. At greater than 500, the ratio is 2 to 1. At over 600, it is 4:1. And at the very highest level, over 700, the ratio of males to females is 13 to 1. The sex differences have become more pronounced with age. The male hormone enhances the visual-spatial skills and female hormones depress them. So the differences in math aptitude become more marked when the boys reach full maturity – a couple of years later than girls. The way the brain was organized in the darkness of the womb creates the mechanism, and the potential, for a specific skill. But the mechanism is only fully activated, and the potential fulfilled, at puberty, when a boy would be expected to join the hunting party.

Adolescent boys tend to develop more confidence, concentration, single-mindedness, channeled aggression, motivation and ambition during this time. This is not acculturation but has been traced directly to the testosterone surge acting on the male brain substrate. Young women, on the other hand, become more acutely aware of the desire to form and maintain closer relationships with people around them.

This hardly needs explaining from the point of view of a million years of child-bearing beginning at this time.

Ideally, everyone would have the opportunity to do what he or she wants to do, and the chance to do it as well as possible. Many people still insist that we are born not just equal, but identical in potential. But we now know that sexual inequalities will persist however much we many wish them away. We ascribe this unequal achievement to basic biology. The brains of each sex are, on the whole, better suited to different tasks.

Something about hormones must further be explained. Something that has been systematically denied since it has only been discovered in the milieu of women's equality. Just as spatial relationship skills are further enhanced and diverge at puberty, the verbal skills of women are enhanced by estrogen. This leads to the unfortunate fact that a girl or woman's test scores on various aptitude tests can vary as much as 14 per cent depending on the time of her monthly cycle. (Again, to repeat myself, a difference of as little as five percent can affect one's educational and occupational opportunities.) The day a young woman takes her SAT can determine her future. Her math scores may be lower if it is a crescendo of estrogen but her verbal scores will be higher. Likewise, during the menstrual phase, when progesterone dominates, her math scores will be higher and verbal scores lower, on average.

In evolutionary terms, this is a relatively modern problem. Prehistoric women, with a shorter reproductive lifespan, and more time spent in nursing their young, could expect a total of ten periods of menstruation in a lifetime. Today's women can expect between three and four hundred – hundreds of months when her emotions, perceptions, sensations and abilities are pulled by the tides of her internal chemistry. Just as legislation to provide equal support to girls and women's sports activities has driven many boy's sports out of existence, at the time when boys need it the most and more than the girls, so women are being limited in what they can have an opportunity to achieve by the unwillingness of being "politically incorrect" enough to incorporate these facts into our schools. On the subject of education and sameness in the name of equality, let's talk about reading and math. Boys remarkably lag behind girls in verbal ability at the time they enter school (based on their DNA). They struggle more at first with the "sit down and shut-up" style of instruction that is standard today. They suffer judgments and assignments (to "slower" classes) as a result, and learn to "hate school" more often as a result. The drop out rate among boys is six times that of girls. This is another example of the lack of recognition and implementation of what is already well known. Recent experiments with separating boys and girls early until they even out have been quite successful and should be spreading like wildfire. Why can't the same thing be done for girls? Their average mathematical skills are not the same as boys so why spawn "math phobia" preferentially among girls? A couple of hours a day of segregated education would be beneficial, not harmful. Of course, this would also allow teachers to respond to the above hormonal cycle of test scores in girls in both math and verbal abilities. Having established segregated classes early, it wouldn't seem so odd to test in segregated groups later. If a woman understands that she is different than a man and how, she can effectively manage the cycles of her ability.

Testosterone results in the single biggest difference between men and women – the innate tendency toward aggression. There is a positive correlation between testosterone levels in the blood and violence in incarcerated men. Testosterone, however, also correlates with dominance and aggression in the every day population, in studies of boys and men in any hierarchal structures. "Alpha males" more often reach the pinnacle of power in their chosen field. In fact, rivalry has been found to increase testosterone levels among the men in competition. Testosterone makes the brain less likely to fatigue, more single-minded. In a male voice choir, basses experienced more ejaculations per week than the tenors. Sixty-nine percent of boys, when confronted with an open conflict, chose aggression. An equal number of same age girls chose avoidance. Scientists have stage-managed a political coup among monkeys by injecting lower order males with extra testosterone.

As I've explained earlier, this and not men's plotting has resulted in the historical dominance of men in society. The pursuit of power is overwhelmingly and universally a male trait. Again, it's in our DNA. That does not mean it's to be used without forethought. However, the tendency is undeniably genetic and normal. We do not teach our boy children to be aggressive, indeed, we try vainly to unteach it. Even researchers most hostile to the acknowledgement of sex differences agree that this is a male feature, and one which cannot be explained by social conditioning. In the past few decades – an evolutionary eyeblink – men have been asked to cool their aggressiveness, share their emotional secrets and be more polite about their sexual thoughts.

There is no longer any question that gender brain differences affect occupation. Men continue to be the majority of society's technocrats, mechanics and inventors. Ninety-nine percent of all patents applied for are registered by men. Women may in fact be ideally suited to be neurosurgeons, given their better fine motor control, but it takes a combination of ability and single-mindedness to reach the pinnacle of such a profession and there are ten men for every woman who really want it. It has been tellingly put that men and women invest their human capital differently. There is often more to life than climbing the corporate ladder for a woman. The breakthrough we have had is that a woman can be anything she wants, if she wants it badly enough. She still may be a small minority in her profession, given the differing tools of evolution, including innate aggression, but the opportunity is there. Likewise, if a man wants to stay home with the kids and be the more nurturing parent, he can too. Make no mistake, however, his style of parenting will be different, colored by his brain characteristics, just as her's will influence how she runs a corporate meeting - or an operating room.

CHAPTER FIVE:

GENDER IDENTITY

I would be remiss if I did not clear up an apparently common misconception here. Gender identity is determined in the womb. A complex formula of male and female hormones, coming on line at certain critical times of fetal brain development, determines to which gender the individual is attracted. Dr. Gunter Dorner has spent his entire career researching this very subject. He now claims to accurately predict potential future homosexual behavior through amniocentesis – that is a sampling of the fluid bathing the fetus, often used to detect Down's syndrome. A very small window (perhaps a week) during the development of a critical area of the brain apparently determines sexual orientation. This is a subtle occurrence in the development of the fetus because homosexual men and homosexual women show the same natural abilities on school testing as the average for their gender and the women still place the same emphasis on fulfilling social relationships. The men tend to value sex over relationship.

Dorner finds that the brain is not masculinized in one simple exposure to male hormones, but in steps over fetal development. It happens in three stages, according to Dorner. The development of what he calls the sex center, then the mating center, and then the gender-role center. First the male hormones (or lack thereof) set to work on creating typical male or female physical characteristics of the body and brain. Later, the brain mating center is developed in a higher area of the brain, the hypothalamus, which controls sexual behavior in adult life.

Male fetuses with lower concentrations of androgen (male hormones) exposure are more likely to seek other males as sexual partners. Females who are exposed to a higher level of these hormones are more likely to be attracted to other females. Finally, Dorner's gender-role center of the brain develops, under similar hormone influence. This center in the brain relates to behavior like level of aggressiveness, or lack of it, individuality or sociability, adventurousness or timidity. These characteristics then get fully expressed under the hormonal influence at puberty.

We are dealing here with fine, critical amounts of testosterone, measured in thousand-millionth parts of a gram. If these levels vary over the course of fetal development one can get virile looking and acting men (sex center) who are attracted to other men (mating center), because of different timing of exposure. One can get homosexual or heterosexual men who are timid or aggressive across a spectrum. The brain is not sexed in one "big bang."

This research is backed up by accidents of nature in the human species. Some men are born with three instead of two sex chromosomes. They may have an extra female chromosome – XXY. They look male, are raised male, but because of the confusing hormone signals during fetal development (they have low testosterone exposure in the womb), they are hesitant about assuming a male role and may become transvestites, transsexuals or bisexuals. The mating center has become befuddled.

Then there are those males who, when studied because their mothers took high doses of therapeutic female hormones, were found to lack general assertiveness, athletic ability and aggression. They often went through life without a long-term sexual relationship, due to their confused mating center.

Of course, this also occurs in females. Girls exposed to high male hormones in the womb, *after* their primary physical sex determination is made, were found to be more frequently bisexual or homosexual and were reported by their mothers to have defied normal gender related play with dolls in favor of the company of competitive boys. Obviously, gender identity and characteristics are the result of a very complex and nuanced hormone interaction in the womb with the fetal brain – hence the array of possible outcomes we observe in society.

What is the cause of these variations in sex hormones in utero? Dorner found that severe stress on the mother during pregnancy more often results in a same sex attracted child. Stress in the mother lowers the male hormone level in the womb. One wonders, from an evolutionary point of view, if this is not a successful adaptation. If stress in the environment of early man – malnutrition, drought, climate change – resulted in fewer children being born to the subsequent generation, one's tribe is more likely to weather the environmental storm. When conditions improve, more grandchildren occur spontaneously.

Knowing all this, of course, begs the question of the "unnaturalness" of homosexuality. It appears to be no more unnatural than left-handedness. It is a biological event, perhaps an adaptation. The principle problem for homosexuals is not of their making. The problem derives from the rest of us – intolerance due to lack of understanding.

(Dorner, G., "Hormones and sexual differentiation of the brain", *Sex, Hormones and Behaviour*, CIBA Foundation Symposium 62.)

CHAPTER SIX:

MID-LIFE

The ages from the end of adolescence (probably 25 in our culture) until approximately forty-five or fifty, is often a relative emotional flatland for men. The stage of emotional maturity, the emotional repertoire, the awareness, that a man reaches by his mid-twenties is often close to what he will have into his mid-forties if he has not had a difficult path. Emotional depth is not an important skill for today's business men. Men don't perceive emotional content as well and therefore "skate" through long periods of life, if unobstructed. Men, relatively, don't value emotional and relationship development, as we have learned from our anthropology lesson and verified with brain research. Linear thinking, focused attention, denial of pain of all kinds, male-based camaraderie, and sex when he can talk someone into it, is a male dream come true. Even marriage and children, to a large extent, don't get in the way of this style of living. We are immersed in our jobs – and when we say a man is immersed in his job – we really mean immersed. It's our main thing. It's our duty. It's our way of taking care of our wife and children. It's our way of showing we love them. We are raising a family. We may be standing on the sideline at our daughter's soccer game but we are too often thinking about work or talking to the guy next to us about the technical aspects of good soccer playing. Remember, these are tendencies that are born into us. We can raise them to choices only through great effort.

However, we forcibly rediscover this emotional terrain, very reluctantly, in our late forties. Why is this? Again, testosterone. At about forty-five to fifty, most men begin to experience some changes for which they are not prepared. Although we may be at the peak of our earning power at work, we are noticeably slowing down physically. Our bodies are changing. We like the status quo. We like order and repetition. We like control. In earlier stages of our lives, testosterone made all the difference. It defined who we were. Now it is redefining. Testosterone levels begin to drop off about thirty-five and reach significantly lower levels as we cross the line into the mid-forties. This shouldn't be a shock when you consider the same primitive strata that we came from. How long did a caveman live? It wasn't until relatively established settlements and then agriculture that people began to survive in significant numbers to "old age" (an age we wouldn't even consider old now). Even in the movies about Native Americans, when the crucial decision-making time of whether to go to war or not is made, sitting around a fire in a teepee, there are only a few older men sitting down. The young bucks are always lobbying for war, standing in the back row. Where are all the other "old" men? They're dead. Only a rare individual, a medicine man or great warrior chief, was supported into old age by the tribe after he stopped killing his own meat. Individuals in primitive hunter-gatherer societies rarely lived past forty-five or fifty.

This was a natural mechanism designed by nature. You slowed down, then you died, one way or the other. Some societies provided mechanisms for men who reached a certain age and first began to feel their physical power waning: they would "stake themselves out" during a battle, meaning they tied themselves to a stake driven in the ground, in order to ensure their death in an honorable way. Cavemen hardly needed these ways of easing themselves out, as death was an early visitor to most of them. They tried to sow their wild oats early and often because death was in the next day's hunt. "Today is a good day to die" may not have been coined by Crazy Horse.

The male body becomes more and more obsolete for the caveman job. Our muscle mass decreases. Our physical reserve is more easily depleted. Our recovery after doing something physical takes longer. Our sexual function changes. Our erections are not as hard or as high. Our refractory period before we can have successful intercourse again is longer. Eventually, our very desire may begin to wane. Testosterone's decline can rob us of our sense of well-being. Without realizing it, we identified with the physical, aggressive nature of ourselves. Now it is being taken away, compromised. We have a tendency to act out. We haven't always developed the deep intimate relationships, even with our significant other, that would allow us to talk about such a core-threatening thing. The red convertible feels good at first but we still don't get the looks from women we want - the look with prolonged eye contact. *She wants me!* is replaced with *Who do I think I'm kidding?* as she turns away.

Or we may look for other ways to reassure ourselves of our potency. We may throw ourselves into our work, looking for some other way to be powerful, or we just get the urge to try some high-risk behavior. Motorcycles are growing in popularity with middle-aged men. We develop an obsession with our golf game, or tennis skills, or it's time to take up sky diving – "Something I have always wanted to do." (We just thought of it yesterday). Anything that restores our feeling of power, of mastery and therefore control becomes attractive. We are under attack with too few arrows in our quiver. Putting our bodies at risk, putting our mental health at risk, putting our primary relationship at risk – nothing is out of the question – because we too often aren't aware of the alternatives. If we go far enough, we will find that "trophy" wife or relationship. Women that will pretend in public that we are all we were at their age, in exchange for other gifts, or "daddy's girls" who are playing the same game as us in reverse. Most of us can't afford these expensive compensations to our ego and they just tend to put off the inevitable anyway. We've lived with blinders on.

Depression

Too often, depression is the mediator. Men go on for years without being diagnosed. The signs overlap almost completely with lower testosterone - less drive, less animation, less sexual desire, less joy, less of everything except a sense of loss. Men commit eighty-one percent of suicides over age sixty. It's not our natural style to talk about it. We often don't even have the verbal aptitude to talk about it when we do realize it. We like to mull things inside until they are solved. This doesn't work with depression. We need to accept outside help, lest we end up as in Shakespeare's *As You Like It*.

"Last scene of all,
That ends this strange eventful history,
In second childishness, and mere oblivion;
Sans teeth, sans eyes, sans taste, sans everything."

(*As You Like It*, Act II, Scene 7)

Sometimes, our women save us. I remember, perhaps fifteen years ago, telling my wife that I was having dreams of standing in the front yard with a shotgun in my mouth. Looking back, I had accomplished every thing I had ever dreamed of (sad to say, nothing involving relationship). I had no concept of what to look forward to next. My relationship with my only son was chronically on the rocks – we were relegated to name-calling at that point. My wife didn't think twice, mince words or act confused. She had me with a psychiatrist within two days.

Alcohol

This is also the time that men most often start to drink too much. Sure, we got drunk when we were young and just learning to drink – seeking risk, having fun. It goes with the personality so typical of men – seeking the rush, the high, the short-term gratification. Then, most of us settled down to drink in moderation in post-adolescence. Alcohol became part of the social scene, the business scene, something to enjoy with or after a ballgame. Too often at mid-life, it is no coincidence, alcohol slowly, insidiously becomes something more - seeking solace. Again, it goes with the personality so typical of men. It is a beautiful and powerful denial mechanism. The high is characterized by grandiosity. What a perfect solution! It is self-reinforcing. We continue to seek, and if it eludes us, to chase the high, the solace, the relaxation, the well-being, often in solitude. The feeling that all is well. We are who we want to be after all. Alcohol becomes our ally, our friend. We seek comfort in it. It fills the surrogate intimate relationship we so desperately need. We are not aware of the desperation, but why would alcohol or drugs become so important if we were not seeking solace, while contemplating the problem. Eventually the solace becomes the solution – and the problem. Alcohol and drugs are the most dangerous solution of all - as dangerous as sky diving without instruction, mountain climbing without a rope.

And it is so sneaky. The next thing we know we are seeking alcohol for it's own sake. We are thinking about it when we are still at work, when we should be doing something else. It can become an obsession. We drink before we go to a party, to "get a head start". Really, it's so other people will not know how much we are drinking and so we don't have to waste time getting high at the start. We will have a sense of well-being when we get there. Suddenly we want to go to cocktail parties! This behavior spawns all kinds of destructive habits, especially dishonesty, with ourselves as well as others. It is a temptation and a necessity. It reinforces denial. It creates false impressions of ourselves as people we are not, and then promotes recurring behavior to support such falsities. It loosens the inhibitions on many other distasteful behaviors that epitomize mid-life crisis.

We are lost souls. Not only are we lost souls, but our culture has galvanized our disorientation. Let me explain.

PART TWO:

THE DILUTION OF MASCULINITY

CHAPTER SEVEN:
TO MAKE MATTERS WORSE

The "Mead Doctrine"

As the women's movement appropriately challenged society to awake overtly to the inequality in the treatment of women, the early theorists looked for support from science. They found it in the writings of Margaret Mead, by then a well-known anthropologist. Mead had concluded that the enormous variability of human behavior in different cultural contexts suggested that innate, or biologically predetermined behaviors were almost non-existent. "We may safely say that many if not all of the personality traits which we call masculine and feminine are as lightly linked to sex as are the clothing, the manners and the form of headdress that a society at a given period assigns to sex." (*Sex and Temperament in Three Primitive Societies*, p. 280.) This "Mead doctrine" was incorporated into a sex/gender system underpinning feminist theory. In this system, the word sex refers to physiological differences in the body, and the word gender to learned behavior in the mind. This two-domain distinction allowed sex-specific bodies to be viewed as separated and distinct from gender-neutral minds, and legitimized the idea that gender specific behaviors and tendencies were essentially completely cultural. Upon this theorem was built the expectation that equal treatment could only be manifest by treating everyone, regardless of gender, the same. Much mischief has been fomented upon this false premise.

THE MYTH OF MALE PATHOLOGY

Social scientists observe that men are more comfortable giving commands. That's because they are more comfortable in hierarchy and direct communication without a fear of offending. Women perceive this as an attempt at domination. Their language tends to feature conditional statements because preservation of the relationship is paramount over "the facts." You recall from the earlier example from *An Accidental Tourist*: As we said, Macon was concerned with the message, the simple matter of the boy's learning math. Muriel is concerned with the "meta-message." What would this say about the relationship, if he began paying for her son's education.

In a recent study, seven married couples were asked to record, on a daily basis, their satisfaction with the relationship. The wives were most satisfied when their husbands verbally expressed affection. The results were found to vary remarkably and were absolutely related to the how affectionate their husbands had been that day. The husbands were most satisfied when their wives acted on their behalf, regardless of words, by looking attractive, cooking and shopping, for instance.

If the brains of humans are gender neutral (as opposed to the rest of their bodies), and this concept is wedded to the notion that women are the model for healthy normalcy in relationships, then maleness becomes a condition desperately in need of a cure. "Maleness has become a 'bad smell' in the room". (Lance Morrow, *A Man's World*, p. 8) Since the two-domain (sex versus gender) distinction requires that we view the behavior of men and women as entirely learned, it was reasonable to assume that the standard for healthy normalcy in love relationships should be the same for both men and women. Since women are more emotionally competent, women have been lifted up as highest "standard" of communication and men have been pathologized as incapable of "proper" communication or intimacy. Because men tend to talk about "things", their friendships and conversations are characterized as superficial and trivial. Since women tend to share feelings, female relationships are celebrated as deep, intimate and true.

Ironically, it has been found, women regard men who defy the masculine norm by disclosing their fears and emotions as "too feminine" and "poorly adjusted." (*Journal of Counseling Psychology*, 37, (1990), pg. 3-9).

EDUCATION

For the first time in history, we are educating girls and boys in a virtually identical manner. The school syllabus reflects and encourages youngsters to believe in the assumption of sameness. As long as childhood education is principally an "I talk – you listen" affair, it will be biased toward females. Little girls will be comfortable in an educational framework where they receive information secondhand, interacting with the teachers and they will ask questions, for that is part of their language apparatus. Little boys, on the other hand, seek to exploit their advantage in seeing. They are less interested in any relationship they may have with the teacher, just as they were less interested in people at one day old, and have a brain bias which makes them curious to explore and find out for themselves.

The female infant's superior babble translates into higher verbal intelligence scores in early childhood. She has discovered, enjoyed, and reinforced the advantage of a better framework for the processing of language, while the boy is still enjoying his more mechanical world of things – their shape, the space they occupy, and how they work. His world is a world of action, exploration and things. But school tells him to sit quiet, listen, not fidget, and pay attention to ideas; everything, in fact, that his brain and body are telling him not to do. The acceptance of verbally communicated information, qualified by question and answer, suits the female mind well. Even manual tasks, such as handwriting, suit the fine motor skills of the female, as opposed to the grosser mechanics of the boy. As Diane McGuinness explains: "Education is almost a conspiracy against the aptitudes and inclinations of the schoolboy. In the early school years, children concentrate on reading and writing, skills that largely favor girls. As a result, boys fill remedial reading classes, don't learn to spell and are classified as dyslexic or learning-disabled four times as often as girls. Had these punitive categories existed earlier they would have included Faraday, Edison and Einstein."

Over 95 per cent of children diagnosed as hyperactive are boys. It is hardly ever diagnosed in girls. Given what we know now about the male/female wiring of the brain, the frustration of boys in early education is not surprising. Again, Dr. McGuinness: "Hiding the knowledge concerning sex-specific aptitudes in learning has done far more harm than good ... it has caused a great deal of suffering in many boys who normally are slower to acquire reading skills. Even more pernicious is the spectacle of young boys on medication for a 'disease' that has no valid diagnosis." Still, while the children already differ in their brain tendencies and aptitudes, great switches in the body are yet to come on, for puberty looms, and with it the discharge and circulation of the sex hormones. The hormonal flow is regulated by that part of the brain which researchers first noticed to be different in men and women – the hypothalamus. So far, we have seen the design and development of two separate engines; now we will see what happens when you add fuel. As children, the hormones set the minds of boys and girls apart in the womb, creating a certain distance between them. Now that distance becomes a chasm. Boys begin to catch up to girls in testing of verbal skills (although not subtleties of communication), and excel in abstract mathematics. Girls become even more focused on relationships – relationships facilitated by communication. Just when boys and girls are attracted to one another, they, in fact, diverge in their understanding of what is important.

As stated previously, the aptitudes for language and math vary considerably in a girl's menstrual cycle. And again, this is a relatively modern problem. While today's adolescent girl and woman can expect cyclic variability in her moods and abilities for decades of her life, and must spend a great deal of energy managing this variability in a society that does not recognize or approve such variation (see "Mead Doctrine").

Currently, up to sixty percent of the students at an average co-educational college or university are female. The majority of bachelors' degrees are now awarded to females in every racial and ethnic group. By 2017, it is predicted, the ratio of female to male college graduates will be one and a half to one. The men who stay in college seek less student leadership positions and perform worse academically than women. Will not these factors, along with the lower graduation rate, promote a "marriage gap?" The world has become more verbal. Yet on average the verbal part of boys brains do not develop to capacity until fourth or fifth grade. The acceleration of formal academic learning has been pushed back earlier in the school curriculum. Reading was once a first-grade challenge. Now some schools expect to see beginning reading skills when a child enters kindergarten. This push has hurt boys far more than girls. The brain scans of verbal skills of girls three and a half years old mirror those of boys 5 years old. Well-meaning parents and teachers who push boys to read and write too early may see their efforts backfiring. Feeling a keen sense of failure, some boys lose interest in learning, an apathy that lasts and limits their efforts later, when their brains catch up with their bodies. In test score achievement accounts reported in the mainstream media, one will find an analysis of racial gaps, income-level gaps, rural/urban gaps, and private school/public school gaps, but seldom an evaluation of gender gaps.

Here are two ideas that are working: One is an urban, co-ed (half black, half white) public elementary school in Delaware, where a program of concentrated one on one tutoring is flourishing. The children may spend three, half-hour sessions each week with a tutor who accepts them where they are, boy or girl. This program has moved the school's ranking from near bottom to the sixth-highest in the state. Last year, one-hundred percent of the boys and 98 percent of the girls passed the state mandated fifth-grade reading test.

Another is in Colorado, where Audra Philippon, principal of AXL, a public elementary charter school in Aurora, divides her boys and girls into same-sex classes from kindergarten on. "They love being alone for learning", says Philippon. Both genders are taught with similar "active-learning" methods. The boys in 2009-2010 are doing just as well as the girls. One would hope this model could include socialization.

Dottie Lamm, former first lady of Colorado has said: "If a men's movement develops for boys, I'll join it. And, as an aging feminist, I'll still fight to take big chunks out of that glass ceiling for women. But as a grandmother of three young boys, I'm going to do my darnedest to keep young boys from sinking into that academic mud floor." (*Denver Post*, July, 2010.)

RELATIONSHIPS

The format of the brain was developed for humans during the time in which they functioned as a hunter-gatherer species. The male brain was more compartmentalized. It was designed to be focused and filter out extraneous data. It was built to be in denial of pain and feelings in submission to an outcome. The female brain was designed to integrate. It drew information linkages from all over both hemispheres to make meaning out of a complex array of non-linear input. So, when the language explosion occurred, it followed the neuronal pathways already laid down. By MRI and PET scans today we see that when asked to perform language based tasks, men's brains are activated on one side only (usually on the left) where the primary language center is located, while women's brains light up on both sides.

Boys want to play with things, and girls want to chat with people. Boys want to achieve and be dominant. The girls will accommodate to this not as a result of some fierce repression, but because most of them are not as interested in reaching the top. Studies of school-age children have shown that, for girls, popularity is more important than success or achievement. This cannot be explained by the theory that clever girls are less popular, because in fact research shows that in girls brain-power is closely associated with social success. More often, the girls expressed a concern for what others thought about them. The boys had begun to define their life aims in terms of the occupations, and the prestige of those occupations, that lay ahead. They were asking, "What is my work to be?", while girls were wondering, "Who will my husband be?"

A woman is more sensitive than a man in her very being. That's because her brain is specialized for this very function. The right hemisphere of her brain that adds emotional content is better connected to the left side of the brain that controls verbal expression than it is in men. The intuitive, if you like, is more in touch with the communicative skills. Girls have spent most of their lives, up to their first serious heterosexual relationship with like-minded people, that is, with people of their own sex. Likewise boys have sought out like-minded people – other boys. When we are thrown together by our hormones, we have no idea what to do with each other. All the things that have worked up until then are null and void. The skills we have honed in the presence of our peers are worthless to us now. Adolescent couples are characterized by this uneasiness. Often, the young men, act-out physically in an attempt to impress the girl. She may look on in horror. Later, the girl may be talking to the boy in animated and somewhat agitated terms. He has a blank look on his face, appearing to wish he was doing anything else.

Women end romantic attachments more often than men. This too, fits in with our knowledge of the female brain. Seeking romance, they can judge the success or failure of romance because relationships are the subject they know and judge best. Women are not the ones blinded by testosterone-fueled desire. They can tell whether or not a relationship is a true and durable one, because they have studied the real nature and value of such a bond. Heartbroken, the man will say how he wants and needs her. Sadly, the woman will know that want and need are no basis for a relationship. Physically, in the female brain, the centers of reason and emotion are better connected. She is better equipped to analyze and rationalize her emotions. Young men fall in love more frequently than women, because their hearts have less communication with their heads – or more accurately, because their brain functions have less communion with each other. Men are less able to understand why women break off a romance, because for them romance itself is more of a mystery. Men try to be romantic by invoking the mental strategy which is more appropriate to them – they do it less by words, than through things. Not for nothing are chocolates and jewelry described as tokens of affection. Not for nothing does he fall for "say it with flowers", since he doesn't know the words. Many men send their loved one a birthday or anniversary card. The trouble arises when it comes to wondering what to write on the darned thing. One man, told by researchers to show more affection towards his partner, decided to wash her car.

Most wives and girlfriends meet great resistance when they try to push their man to talk about feelings. They often come to the conclusion that the men in their lives are afraid of expressing emotion. Nearly three-quarters of the women in long-term relationships or marriages have stated in studies to have finally given up trying to achieve a closer emotional bond. Eight out of ten say men often seem not really to hear in a way that captures what she is trying to say, when asked to report the content of a conversation. About forty percent of women say their male partner often tells them not to feel what they are feeling, or at least not to express it. The conventional explanation is that men are conditioned not to acknowledge their feelings – the "big boys don't cry" syndrome.

Numerous studies have shown that men feel closest to other people (men and women) when working or playing side by side. Women feel closest to other women when talking face to face. It is to be expected that women would try to duplicate that feeling with their significant other male. These differences in "preferred cognitive strategy" can be frustrating.

When men comfort one another during a crisis, such as the loss of a loved one, it is with physical presence rather than talk. Often few words are exchanged. Men use action phrases to describe feelings of depression, such as "running on empty", or "running in place". Women, when clinically depressed, want to talk about their feelings and can do so more accurately.

Now we know that the reluctance men have with feeling and with communicating emotions has a biological root. Men's capacity to feel is, to a greater degree than in women, physically divorced from their capacity to articulate. The emotional centers of the male brain are located far more discretely than in the woman. It's not that he bottles things up. It is more that his emotions are in a separate box, in a separate room, a room not routinely visited. Holding a door open, or carrying in the groceries is not a mere social convention. It is the masculine way of saying "I care for you." The most common reason listed for divorce is "lack of communication." But it's in the genes, not the attitude. He may not know how he feels or, if he does, how to say it.

CHAPTER EIGHT:
PRACTICAL BEHAVIOR

Joe Tanenbaum, from whom I borrowed the illustration in the Prelude, in his lectures and subsequent book, *Male and Female Realities: Understanding the Opposite Sex,* has studied the human species from a different perspective – that of behavior – and drawn the same conclusions, stated in different words.

EMOTIONAL STYLES

Men have two well-developed modes of perception – useful for the last several million years. These modes of perception are the (compartmentalized) intellectual and the physical (action). Men are built to create intellectual constructs in their minds. Often, if a problem cannot be solved immediately and linearly, it will be put on the back burner, "mulled" as he would say, until a solution presents itself. This mulling process may last minutes or decades, coming up occasionally to be rethought. This "mulling" technique is the process that drives women crazy. He appears to not be attending to what she is saying. He is not making eye contact and appears not to be listening. He is working on the problem, whether it is something left over from work or something he was presented with on arriving home. She wants conversation. She wants to "explore" the issue in open conversation - her preferred style. He appears to be shutting down. He is not comfortable with speech without thinking first.

If a problem proves or appears to be insoluble, men have only two other choices, that they are most comfortable with, to deal with the issue. They can go to "physical (action) mode" and begin to act upon the problem. This can take productive or destructive forms. They can apply a bigger tool and increased leverage (straining in one way or the other) until the "bolt" moves, for better or for worse. In another form, they can become aggressive towards the environment or other people, letting off steam and expressing their frustration and possibly getting movement that is helpful. This tends to work much better with other men than with women. With women it can be domestic violence.

Unfortunately, the other alternative when a problem seems intellectually insolvable and is not amenable to action, is "stuffing" it. Men think our bodies should be impervious to pain. In fact, men do bear acute pain better, even reveling in it, than women who wisely tend to avoid it. Storing pain, therefore, in the body, brings him a funny sort of resolution. Since we want our bodies to be impervious to pain, and we can't imagine ourselves past forty-five, we think it will never come back to haunt us. And it feels a lot better than continuing to watch it percolate on the stove, when we don't see a solution. The result is that stress-related diseases are male-dominated – heart attacks, ulcers, substance abuse and suicide. These are our bodies coming back to haunt us because we didn't die appropriately for our currently evolved form and we had no better coping mechanism than the dumping ground/ out of sight storage area that we call our bodies. Our bodies are what we trust the most – why not dump it there? It was a good evolutionary strategy for a million years when life was short. The fact that those days are gone makes it no less neurochemically driven, no less cellular, no less inherent in our genes.

Women have a bit larger array of ways to express themselves. The intellectual and physical are still there, but a well-honed emotional repertoire is at their fingertips as well. They can talk about it, cry, laugh, be sad, be glad, be mad, be ambivalent and a hundred shades and combinations of those choices. They usually have a network of other people that they have a long history of having cultivated for such purposes. Men expect to deal with things immediately or take them to the grave. There is only one reason for a man to talk about something – because he can no longer contain it. It has overwhelmed his intellectual toolbox and overpowered his defenses. He is out of control! Talking about it is his last resort. Nothing feels scarier to a man than being out of control. He will do anything, even talk about it to a woman, to regain control over himself. Hence, the frustration expressed by women when they try to get men to talk about their feelings, when there is obviously something bothering them. First of all, men are not in touch with their emotional realm, so "I don't know" is often an honest answer. Women often interpret this as stone-walling or stubbornness. Women live in an emotional world all day long, so from their perspective, to say "I don't know how I feel" is absurd. Men must be either afraid or unwilling to share their feelings. Second of all, a man would rather die than reveal that he can't figure something out and is feeling out of control. "Just give me some time" is an appropriate response from the male brain, as he continues to mull the problem or prepares to stuff it. During these times he will appear to be emotionally unavailable. But he is working hard. It is all internal. Often he will need a place to "hole up" during this time. The emotions associated with a situation are not a part of the equation. When they are, he feels out of control. He is trying to suppress them. He is not taught to tune them out, he was born to ignore them. That's as far as his repertoire goes.

So, you can see that when a woman presents a problem to a man, with all of her emotional embellishments, he can only draw one conclusion. She is out of control and needs help immediately to regain control. She is desperate for a solution. She is begging for help (as he would be if the tables were turned). Of course, she may be just enjoying herself – floating trial balloons of different possibilities, trying to exchange emotional information, wallowing in the joy of her emotional competence. This is bliss for her. This would be (and often is) hell for him. So she may not enjoy him interrupting her with solutions. He thinks he is doing the loving thing. It would be if he were in her shoes. Hence the "battle of the sexes" is all a misunderstanding of different dynamics. Both men and women are doing what they perceive to be the loving thing for each other – her sharing emotional information, him reassuring her that there is a solution. Until we accept the fact that we have developed differently and that this has profoundly affected how we perceive what is going on, and what we are meaning to say to each other, we will continue to look at each other as if we are lying creatures from another planet.

INTELLECTUAL STYLES

A man asks a woman: "Do you know the way to the restaurant?" She says "yes." She is driving. They set off joyfully, looking forward to the evening. When they get to the end of the block, she hesitates a beat, looks both ways, then says: "Now which way is it, left or right?" The man clenches his jaw. As far as he's concerned she has just lied to him. To him, knowing the way to the restaurant means A to B to C to D to E. To her it may mean, "I've been there before: I'm sure I can find it." She will use many cues to help her along the way and will eventually arrive at the restaurant, triumphantly pulling into the parking lot. However, they are no longer speaking. She interprets his directions in "that tone of voice", as an attempt to dominate her. He thinks he is just doing them both a favor since she *obviously* does not know the way to the restaurant. These two conflicting ways of doing things are in our genes. One is not more right than the other. They are meant to complement one another. We can learn to trust one another if we just realize, understand and accept that this is true – that we are different. Then a man can say to himself at the first street corner. "It's OK, she'll find the restaurant. This is just her way of doing it," and they arrive with no conflict. Likewise, a woman can ask a man "What's going on" but if he isn't ready to talk about it, say "Let me know when you are ready to talk about it." This frees him up to mull to his hearts content but empowers him (makes him feel more comfortable with) doing exactly what she asks, because he's not being pushed. It's not an out of control situation. The more we know about each other's styles, the more we respect them, the better the relationship communication.

Because men have only two preferred options, the physical and the intellectual, they of course, interpret all attempts to communicate through these modes. Presenting them with a nuanced emotional question, leaves them either flummoxed or trying to "figure it out" intellectually. Women want to be heard. They may not want to come to a resolution, or may decide after some discussion whether they even need a resolution. Men can't wait that long. To them the hypothetical discussion is absurd. She should be putting it on the back burner or taking his suggested solutions. Why else bring it up? And still the woman is talking – she suddenly realizes that he has tuned her out. He can't stay with her that long.

Of course, we modern men have learned to not appear as clueless

as we really are. After all, we were raised by women. So we often say
– "I hear you", or "I understand" or "oh yeah" or "wow", when we
clearly *don't* understand and have tuned the conversation out long ago
to protect ourselves from the energy drain. Conversation energizes
women. For men, they feel like they are having the energy sucked right
out of them. It's self-preservation for men to tune out and lie about it.
Women want something from us that we are not comfortable with –
emotional conversation. We want something back from women, so we
learn to fake it. Some of us are very good at it. However, women often
detect that we really aren't getting it, even though we swear that we are.
They walk away feeling frustrated, unsatisfied, incomplete and call one
of their girlfriends to men bash. They think we are faking it (we are)
because we don't care. Nothing could be further from the truth. We
are straining to stay focused and appreciate the importance our women,
apparently, place on what they are saying, but we just don't get it. It's
a mystery. Just like – "How can a man not know how he feels?" "It's
nuts! It's impossible!" No, it's just us. Believe me, it's as frustrating for
men as it is for women. There is the co-universal human nature that
has developed over millions of years of evolutionary history, driven by
survival selection, that has given males and females different natures,
based on the challenges we have faced as genders. If we accept the
knowledge that we are perceptually so different, and begin to explore
it together, we can create some options. But these options will still be
expressed through the brains that we live with, the bodies that we live
in. For that reason, it's about time we become familiar and at ease with
our differences.

Evolutionary psychology leads us to understand that humans are
adapted to a way of life that has served us well for 99 percent of human
history. If males and females have children they'd better be prepared to
raise them. Children need fully gendered fathers and mothers. Elders
are needed to parent the parents. And men and women need not live in
a world where the battle of the sexes rules our lives, but can live in one
where differences can be appreciated. The way home is not to decry our
differences, or have us believe that they don't exist, but to create a world
where differences can be honored and appreciated as *good*. The starting
point on a new relationship age is learning to trust each other, even
though we don't understand each other. Assume that the other gender is
telling the truth. Respond from that point of view even though it makes

no sense to us. Take it at face value and respond as if you can trust it. If we both act accordingly, we are in for a lot of discoveries.

> *"Raging at men's innate maleness is as useful as raging against the weather, or the existence of the Himalayas. We believe it is rather more sensible to put on a raincoat, and abandon plans to bulldoze Everest."*
>
> (*Brain Sex*, pg. 128)

CHAPTER NINE:

PROBLEMS WITH THE "MEAD DOCTRINE"

As you recall, we have been operating out of an old paradigm, developed before we had actual brain anatomic and physiologic data on gender differences. This paradigm, based on an eminent anthropologist, Margaret Mead, is based on the assumption that while men and women are physically different and distinct, their brains are not. The human brain was assumed to be gender neutral. Now that we know that this is not true, what shall we do? This belief, of a gender neutral brain, is the foundation of the last forty years of attempts to create gender neutral relationships, marriages, work places and schools. We now know that we as men, and we as a society, have to try something different. Let me introduce what I believe to be the solutions.

PART THREE:

THE SOLUTION

**Reclaiming our Manhood
"Welcome Back, Brother"**

CHAPTER TEN:
GETTING TO KNOW ONESELF AS A MAN

> *"We are living in an important and fruitful moment now, for it is clear to men that the images of adult manhood given by the popular culture are worn out; a man can no longer depend on them. By the time a man is thirty-five he knows that the images of the right man, the tough man, the true man, which he received in high school do not work in life. Such a man is open to new visions of what a man is or could be."*
>
> —Robert Bly, *Iron John*, Preface, ix.

I want to make clear that this book does not seek to turn men against women, or to return men to a macho mode. Women and their values are a blessing to us all. The grief in men has been increasing steadily since the start of the Industrial Revolution and the grief has reached a depth now that cannot be ignored. The male in the past twenty years has become more thoughtful and more gentle. But by this process he has not become more free. He is a nice boy who pleases not only his mother but also the young woman with whom he is living. Thirty years ago, at the onset of the woman's movement, women were saying that they definitely preferred these softer, more receptive males. "Women Say Yes to Men Who Say NO!" was a Vietnam era bumper sticker, encouraging conscientious objection. As we have seen, however, multiple studies now show that women, while not necessarily realizing the instigation of this change in men, have become less enamored with men solely in touch with their feminine side.

Part of the grief men feel arises out of a remoteness from their fathers, from the sacred masculine. The fathers of the Fifties understood their role to be aggressive, never cry and always provide. They were gone much of the time to work at a site distant from their home. When they were home, they were emotionally unavailable. Women were not appreciated for their depth or values but primarily for their bodies. This is the male that spawned the beat generation and hippie era of rebellion as the boys and girls of that era had missed their father's presence. A generation off the farm, with absentee fathers and a lack of male mentors, had loosed the dogs of war on society. This is the male that spawned the women's movement as well.

Now men have learned, in this vacuum of authentic male presence, to be the gentler, softer, more receptive male. They have lost the thread of what it is like to be fully a man. However, the grief we see in men crying all over the country is more than just the loss of their fathers. It is partly too, grief formed from trouble in their relationships with women. They had learned to be receptive, but receptivity wasn't enough. In every relationship something fierce is needed once in a while. Both men and women need to have it. But the young men have so valued nurturing that they have lost touch with their fierceness. In The Odyssey, Hermes instructs Odysseus that when he approaches Circe, who represents a certain kind of matriarchal energy, he is to lift or show his sword. Many men now days can't lift or show their sword, for fear of hurting someone. But showing one's sword doesn't necessarily mean fighting. Catching the light of the sun on one's drawn sword, setting a boundary, shows one's decisiveness, and can be a joyful display. "I can ask for what I want and stick by it", it states. Robert Bly, in his book *Iron John*, speaks of the third possibility for men, neither macho nor passive - a man who possesses the full spectrum of responses. A man who is in touch with his "Wild Man" as well as his feminine side and can chose alternatively, as needed, which tool to bring to bear, for the benefit of all involved. The Wild Man is that part of our innate maleness that I have described in the research on male and female brain. He represents, in the ancient myth of Iron John, the ability inherent in every man to assert himself, establish and defend his boundaries, and compete and kill his enemies if necessary. In this day and age, the killing is hopefully symbolic or psychological, but still just as necessary. A boy may need to "kill" the image of his father given to him by his mother. He may need to kill the image of what he is supposed to be in order to make women happy. He may need to fight for what, in his heart, he knows is true and right for him. In the ancient mythical story of *Iron John*, the Wild Man does not hurt anyone, is not violent in any way, but he is assertive in demanding his freedom. He knows when he is trapped. He is a frightening figure to behold. His image promises the potential for physical assertion if his words are not enough. The boy has to find the Wild Man and embrace that part of him, while understanding that the Wild Man is not in charge. The Wild Man is channeled by the boy who is breaking free of childish images of himself and finding his manhood. Forever after, he knows that he can show his sword if he has to.

Many men feel the loss of this ability but they don't understand it. In trying to heal this wound, they turn to their inner feminine, which is what they have been taught to do, to find it. It isn't there. Most men want some nice person, usually a woman, to return their inner gold, their innate self value. But a man will not find his inner power in the force field of an Asian guru or a gentle Jesus. Men are living in captivity now; keeping their Wild Man in a cage. Jesus came out of his gentleness, was baptized by a hairy man and went off resolutely on his Hero's journey. With determination, he was "all in." He had recaptured the essence of the Truth and set out to bring it back to the consciousness of his world. In order to do that, he had to let his "Wild Man" out of his cage. He had to take him with him on the road. Without him he wouldn't have made it to his goal. He wouldn't have transformed the world.

Like most mothers, his' probably dreamed of "My son the Doctor," "My son the Rabbi," "My son the gentle lover of his wife." Few mothers dream of "My son the Wild Man." But if they are lucky enough to find it in their husbands – then they want it for their sons. Women know, however, that in the act of claiming their wild man, their sons are irretrievably separating. So, they often unconsciously discourage it, clinging. This is the natural place for the male presence to step in and pull the boy into manhood.

Ancient societies believed that a boy became a man only through ritual and effort. They believed that it occurred only through the active intervention of older men. The father often is in no position to do this. He has no work to share with his son. It is the work of the elders, the grandfather perhaps. In the Navajo culture, it has traditionally been the uncle's role. Priests and medicine men have become part of the system supporting the nuclear family in our age, not agents of initiation. Last century, the grandfathers lived at home or on adjacent land. Now they live in Arizona, Florida or the old folk's home. Most boys' main companions are other boys – their teachers – older boys who know nothing at all. Fortunately, when necessary, a woman can facilitate the necessary separation from her son, on her own. I say "fortunately" because so many single mothers exist today. It takes awareness and resolution. It takes courage. It may involve sending him to his father for longer and longer periods, if the father is not a truly evil man. He may not be "nurtured" there, so it is scary. Each time he returns he is a little more a man. All over the country now we see hulking sons acting ugly in the kitchen and talking rudely to their mothers. They intuitively know that they must achieve separation to be healthy and they are attempting to make themselves unattractive to their mothers. It's time for a *man* to take them away for a time. Too often, a boy's only other significant adult relationship is with a school teacher, most often a woman.

C.G. Jung said that when a son is introduced to "feeling" primarily by his mother, he will learn the female attitude toward masculinity and take a female view of his father. Often she says "Your father can't help it." So the son grows up with a wounded image of the father – not necessarily brought about by his father's words or actions but based on the mother's observations of those words or actions, which she doesn't understand. When a woman confides in a boy too early, cultivating him as a surrogate partner, he learns shame. He can never fulfill her wish for him to be a substitute kinder, gentler husband.

Often it is at the time of early mid-life, when we begin to yearn for our "real" fathers. We have come to realize that our mother's interpretation is not serving us any more. Robert Bly tells of a friend who, at about thirty-five, began to wonder who his father really was. He hadn't seen him in ten years. He flew out to where he lived, knocked on the door, and when his father opened it, said, "I want you to understand one thing. I don't accept my mother's view of you any longer."

His father broke down in tears, and said, "Now I can die." His son had come back to find a relationship with him. The father had been waiting.

I'm not saying that all fathers are good. A mother may be right about the father's negative traits. But she can be judgmental about masculine traits out of misunderstanding too. The Hindus offer Shiva as an image of masculinity, who is both an ascetic and a good lover, a madman and a husband. He is the god-man, like the unsanitized Jesus, who models responsible masculine behavior. In his fierce form, he can be very dangerous. In his enlightened form he can be incredibly wise. What we call Christ is the fully recognized form of the man Jesus. When Jesus goes wild in the temple, whipping the money changers, many people don't understand. They don't want to deal with the meaning. He is being a man. He sees evil and is outraged. He does what needs to be done with a flair. He is not afraid of his anger or afraid to express it. When a man gets in touch with his wild man, he may shout and take action on behalf of all. It can be scary. Women often fear violence. But such a man finds true strength. He does not pick on the weak. It may be good that the divine is associated with the Buddha, the Virgin Mary and the blissful Jesus. However, imagine how different it would be for young men, as in other cultures, to also associate the divine with mad dancers, fierce hairy men and heroes willing to show their swords. These men honor women. The ability of a male to shout, perhaps out of joy, or set a boundary - show his sword so to speak - does not imply domination, treating people as objects or demanding land or empire. Some people make no distinction between the instinct for fierceness and the instinct for aggression. Women got in touch with their fierce energy in the Sixties and Seventies. Men need to make a parallel connection with the energy the Hindus call Kala. Connecting with this Kala energy will have the effect of meeting this same energy in women (called Kali). If we men don't do that, we won't survive as males. Men are suffering right now – young men and middle-aged men especially. Hopefully not every man will have to be driven to plumb the depths of his psyche by his grief over his self-denied masculinity. Hopefully, we will all come to realize what we have lost, men and women alike, and the road back to the male capable of fierceness as well as gentleness will be taken.

HOW DO WE GET IT BACK?

We think now of our older boys. Our society produces a plentiful supply of boys, but seems to produce fewer and fewer men. Male adolescence is a time of risk-taking, courting danger, going out to the edge. Adolescent wildness and its challenge to our ideas, through their music, their fashions, their words, their codes, announce that the initiatory moment has come. In Western society, heavy metal and rap music lyrics are like boys talking ugly to their mothers, and all society. They need push back. They are seeking initiation. They are seeking wounds. Unfortunately, too often their "gang" or their girlfriend provides the criteria and the experience that he is seeking.

What wound do we have that still requires recognition, the application of balm? Not receiving a blessing from one's father is such a wound. Some men wait all their lives for their fathers to say they love them. Having an absent, a remote, a workaholic father is such an injury. Having a critical, judgmental father is such a wound. Some wound normally comes from our father. Something we can recall for years. An angry blow, verbal or otherwise, that cuts us to the quick. Being lied to by older men is such a blow. When the young men arrived in Vietnam and Iraq, and found that they had been lied to, they received immeasurably deep wounds, as evidenced by the psychological damage manifested by them compared to earlier wars. Never having been welcomed into the male world by older men is a wound. Some boys not only don't have a responsible man at home, they have never met one. Their rage at these circumstances spills over on all authority figures; teachers, police and anyone who would ordinarily be a potential mentor. Not having a soul union with other men can be the most damaging wound of all.

Men have lived in communities with heart unions and soul connections for millions of years. Men have the same brain-driven urge to strive toward a goal in modern society, but they do it in isolation. Now, the isolated male's major emotions are anxiety, tension, loneliness and fear. His lover, usually a woman, is his soul mate. He stops after work to have light conversation over light beer, with other men, seeking something he knows not what. Then he goes home to his sublimated life and wonders: *Is this all there is?* At the same time, his wife is thinking the same thing.

The solution to this is to turn his woundedness, his grief, into an asset rather than a trap. Too often boys attempt to rise above their wound with grandiose behavior. Our Wall Street traders, irresponsible bankers and lenders and many political leaders have been an all too obvious example of the former – above the law and without apparent ethics. Rules are for other people; like a gang without elders. These men have never grown up. They don't know what stepping into responsible leadership is. Like Narcissus, separated from his hunting party and with Hera mad at him, sitting pensively by a pool, he looks into the water and falls in love with himself. Being separated, isolated, Narcissus had no one to guide him, to help integrate the experience he was undergoing.

Alternatively, a man can chose to take on the identity of his wound and become the victim – acting out his childhood daily. Depression, addiction and shame, numbness and paralysis are the signs of this path. A hollowness at the center is the overwhelming feeling. The man cannot find a mentor or be honest about his feelings because he is unworthy. Too many American men follow one of these roads, Narcissus or victim, instead of facing their feelings from childhood.

Initiation rites and male camaraderie discouraged both grandiosity and victimhood. These feelings are the portal through which we become authentic. Anger will rise up. We get in touch with the fierce determination that is within all of us. We learn to act responsibly. We learn to love ourselves. We will be asked to assume responsible leadership, first for ourselves, then for others. Among the Native American (Seneca) tribe, the chief, a man, was chosen by the women. He accepted power for the sake of the community. He himself owned virtually nothing. All the great cultures except ours preserve and have lived with the images of this positive male power. There is a general assumption now that every man in a position of power is or soon will be corrupt and oppressive. Yet the Greeks understood and praised this positive male energy that has accepted leadership authority. They called it "Zeus energy" which encompassed intelligence, compassion, decisiveness, good will, and generosity. Zeus energy is male authority accepted for the sake of the community. The Judeo-Christian tradition is replete with such men: Noah, Abraham, Solomon, David, Jacob, Jesus. Their life was not their own. It belonged to the community they served.

At about the age of forty-five I began to feel this yearning to experience male energy. I purposely moved geographically closer to my parents and consciously started a reapproachment with them. I began to go on little fishing trips with my father. These grew into more shared activities. It was natural to discuss things around the campfire, cooking stove or a game or three of cribbage that we had never shared when I was a boy. I had been "off to college" for a long time.

I came to know my father as a man. I came to understand and respect the decisions he had made and what he had done with his life – what he had seen as his duty. In his own way, he had been "all in", trying to be a good husband and provider. He had never spoken of it. I came to realize how much he loved me even though he never said it. After my father become too old and ill to go on these trips, I went fishing once by myself, driving the same battered camper. On the way home I cried so hard I had to pull over. The sense of loss was overwhelming. I don't remember crying as much at my mother's funeral, even though she largely raised me due to my father's perpetual absence. Having learned my opinion of my father from my mother, the reality of who he was surprised me in many ways. I believe all men need to throw off indoctrination and begin to discover for themselves what a father is and what masculinity is. If I wanted to get a straight picture, I needed to go to the source. He wasn't available when I was young. Fortunately, I was able to learn later. I no longer believed "Your father can't help it."

The alternative is denial. Denial means we have been entranced. We live for years in a trance. Most often we need to be helped out of this trance, to find the gold within us that is our birth right. It is then we find what we are really good at, our mission in life. The young runner crosses the finish line in the presence of his coach: his feet feel as if they are gold. The physicist working with his mentor suddenly writes an equation on the board with his golden chalk. Good gardeners have gold thumbs, not green ones. Sometimes the mentor/teacher, sitting with a student, slips into soul water and his tongue turns to gold. Finding these gifts resulted from a wound that hurt so much we had to dip it in that soul water. Where a man's wound is, there will his genius be. To the Roman's the word genius meant, literally, the divine spark in every person. A true man keeps walking, dragging his guts behind him, looking for the sacred pool. Others point the way. Wherever the wound appears in our psyches, whether from alcoholic father, shaming mother, or shaming father; whether it stems from disability, disease or isolation; that is precisely the place from which we give our major gift. Seeking the sacred masculine, ancient stories are a good help because they are free of modern psychological and cultural prejudices. Mythology adds weight to the wound. These stories have endured centuries of scrutiny from men and women. They give both the light and dark side of manhood. They model not the perfect man but the wounded man who struggles with his own limitations. David, in the Bible, sends Bathsheba's husband off to the front lines to die. He is selfish with desire, yet this does not preclude him from being a great king for his people. Like him, we will not be perfect, but will seek the Truth and the greater good, confessing our sins to one another.

Jesus set out on his mission with resolute determination. Truth had been subverted by the power and dominance of the establishment men of the time – much as it is today. Today money buys elections in the United States, and in turn policy. These are the same money changers that Jesus drove from the temple. For me, this adds new meaning to: "He died for our sins" - the sins of recurring generations. We have again lost the thread of Truth. Do we need to fight to reclaim our right of self-determination? Do we need to be willing to go to the cross, in some sense? Or are we waiting to be rescued - waiting for a man like Jesus to step into the crucible, again, in our place. We have ample signposts, laid out by the great men before us. What we need is a little fierceness, resolution, willingness to do what ever is required.

There is an inherent value in this needed masculine energy. Violence only follows fear in those whose power is threatened. Gandhi and Martin Luther King pursued peaceful resistance with the same kind of fierceness that we revere in George Washington and Abraham Lincoln, who were forced to fight wars of assertion. There is an old saying in biology: "Ontogeny recapitulates phylogeny." What this means literally is that the life of a creature restates all the evolution of his or her species up to that time. Hence, a human embryo goes through stages with gill slits, amphibian and reptilian organs and a primitive brain before finally topping it all off with the "latest thing", at the end of fetal development. Likewise, knowing the evolution of the human brain, I would propose that this applies to our behavior as well. Boys often like to make bows and arrows and hunt or pretend to hunt or fight with guns and fists. They may even bring home a dead animal to their horrified mother.

We often try to educate them out of this primordial behavior, going to great lengths in ethical discussion, explaining our position. But a boy is just living out his history as a male. It doesn't mean he is going to kill things forever. Like the gill slits, the urge is exchanged for something new. Ancient man learned about God and nature through hunting. Shaming a boy about acting out his natural instincts may result in his getting "stuck" there, still bringing a deer back to Detroit on the top of his car at fifty. I suspect more wars have been started on this basis than not. The fierceness I'm taking about does not equate to violence. It is Martin Luther saying, "Here I stand, I can do no other."

Everything I say about men has a parallel in women. I talk about men because I don't "know" a woman's state. Also, men are generally so much less aware of who they are and what they need. I am going to let women take care of themselves. If men are to successfully make the transition to second adulthood, gaining depth of self-knowledge is crucial.

Having dragged our guts there, looking into the sacred pool, we see not just who we thought we were, but another man, not easily included under the name our parents gave us; Edward or Lance or Kerry. Looking into these eyes we see some other being we may have never met. The Gnostics spoke a great deal about the twin, who they imagined to have been separated from us at birth. The twin, when he or she reenters the psyche, insists on intensity and seriousness. Again, Robert Bly tells of a man, who while meditating, saw a man of light at the end of the corridor, nine feet tall and holding a spear. The man of light walked up and said, "If you don't make something of life, I will take it from you." The man was 38 years old when he had this vision.

The eyes looking back at us from the pool are the eyes of our unspoken feelings. We are hoping for resources while looking into this scary pool. These eyes are also the eyes of the Other. They represent the intelligence in nature and the universe, an emblem of consciousness "out there", God if you like. We are looking into the eyes of God when we look into our soul. We find allies in ourselves, mythology and a Higher Power that makes sense of things.

The Native American culture saw the animals as equals. There were the Bear tribe and the Buffalo tribe. When the hunters hunted, doing their share of the ritual, the buffalo tribe participated in the hunt too. It seems that the Native Americans saw this part animal, part human, part god, with their inner eyes. It seems clear, looking at the animals depicted in the Dordogne caves of France, that these artists had seen them also. They had learned the difference between secular space and ritual space. Ritual space gives something back to the man or woman who, prepared by discipline and effort, enters it.

So, a boy has "choices." He can become the grandiose Narcissus. He can become the self-absorbed victim. He can be resolutely led into his appropriate masculinity by rising up and insisting on his own sacred, unique path to identity. He does this by accepting an initiatory task(s). In past days, these were given to him by his father as they worked together in the fields, or his grandfather. He earned his right to be among the men by his actions. We deduce that accepting this task is more important than succeeding or failing at it. The elder's job is to teach the young man how abundant, various and many-sided his manhood is. His body and his brain inherits physical abilities developed long ago by long dead ancestors. If he is lucky, he is given the context by which to turn this process into an identity that honors him and that serves the greater good. The job of the initiator is to prove to the boy that he is more than mere flesh and blood - to affirm a sense of splendidness, a sense of blessedness. The young person is lifted up into what is great in him.

The boy child, having been nurtured up until now, sees, experiences, the inner energy – his Wild Man. He begins to seek to lose his innocence. He let's the Wild Man out in order to seek healthy separation. He has to break with his learned self-image. He has to find himself. He lives with his Wild Man long enough to receive the gifts that allow him to function in the world as a man. He learns to trust his instinctual body. He learns that there is something in reality greater than himself. He has felt, with adolescence, the mental and physical abilities he had never imagined. Each of us has already guessed that we are the sons of kings and queens that somehow landed mistakenly in our dumb, prosaic family. Going out into the world, we get different feedback. We are, then, in danger - lacking initiation and proper grounding - of falling into delinquency, addiction and self-shaming. Or, we can become "flying boys", Peter Pan or "The Little Prince", like so many of our men today, lacking the ability or willingness to accept responsibility or commitment. Young men need a task. They need to become successful at something before they reach adolescence with all its dangers. When

Jung, out of his great understanding of the masculine archetype and its need to be realized, established a training center in Zurich, he would only accept men who were already established in another field. They often started with him at or after thirty-five. Now boys go off to college and sometimes finish without the slightest sense of the limitations of necessity in their parents lives. After graduating, their parents assume that they will go out and find a job and make a life for themselves, having sacrificed to give them the tools to do so. Instead, the boys come back home and make no effort toward moving out of the nest. They have never been apprenticed to a real job, initiated into manhood. They have no work ethic.

Of course, some young men take on responsibility too early, commit to supporting others and carry tremendous burdens. Their family tradition may be that the son's grandiosity should be wiped out early. He has no right to look up, to the see the sun, the light. Men need to be admired, by each other and by women, for their activity. Once, men and women alike expected men to pierce the dangerous places, do the heavy and dangerous work, strain against the tide, and guard the flock at night. Now the boars run wild in the stockyard, the world in full of dangerous places, and the biggest threat to women comes from uninitiated boys. For hundreds of thousands of years men dared to enter the realm of animals, learned their dances, understood and respected their ways. Some men, we called shamans, entered the spirit world of the collective soul, seeking and finding themselves and their mission. They learned the ways of the larger creation, known by different names, all meaning God, and were thereafter able to save people who had become ill through their astonishing knowledge and initiative.

Now, men have been asked to learn how to go with the flow, how to follow rather than lead, how to live in a non-hierarchical way, how to be vulnerable, how to adopt consensus decision-making. Some women want a passive man, if they want one at all. The church wants a tamed man – they are called priests. The university wants a domesticated man – they are called tenure-track people. The corporation wants a "team worker." Passivity increases exponentially as the education system turns out "products." The average American teenager has seen four thousand hours of commercials, yet very few televisions have axes buried in them. The infant boy struggles against his father's narcissistic attempt to murder him; struggles against swaddling bonds; and fights his mothers desire to control him. When the boy fails to get free, then, he learns to sulk. How often an adult man, when baffled by a woman's peculiar interpretation of his behavior – so different from his own understanding – goes into a sulk. It may last for days. It may build upon other wounds and confusion that are not yet acted upon.

If no old men appear to break the hold of the sulking infant, regardless of its age, the habit of passivity becomes entrenched and spreads. He goes into a robot mentality at work. He skips over parenting. He is angry but does not allow himself to express it. He becomes passive in his relationship with his spouse. A woman does not want a man to tell her what to do, but she surely doesn't want to have to always tell him what to do. Lack of initiation leads to lack of initiative.

We see more and more passivity in men, but also more naiveté. The naïve man, as Robert Bly sees him, feels a pride in being attacked. If his wife or girlfriend, furious, shouts that he is just being such a "man", he just takes it. He feels, as he absorbs attacks, that he is doing the brave and advanced thing. He will surely recover somewhere in isolation. A woman, so mysterious and superior, has given him some attention. To be attacked by someone you love – what could be more wonderful? Perhaps the wounds will allow him to remain special a little longer. He is proud that he can pick up the pain of others. He particularly picks up women's pain. When at five years old, he sat at the kitchen table, his mother may have confided her suffering to him, and he felt flattered to be told of such things by a grown-up, even if it showed his father poorly. He later becomes attracted to women who share their pain. His specialness makes him, in his own eyes, something of a healer. He will offer to carry a woman's pain before he checks with his own heart to see if this labor is good and proper for him.

I don't mean that men shouldn't listen. But there is a difference between listening and seeking to carry someone else's pain. It doesn't work well for the carrier in the long run. In his special relationship, he may think that if he doesn't explore the other's dark side, they won't explore his. The pathology will go unchallenged and called good, in fact, superior. Such people have no soul. Their soul mate carries their soul. He assumes that his good will should protect him from the consequences that fall to lesser people. He may eventually say to his irate mate, who is emboldened and enraged by his capitulation, "You're right. I had no right to do that." Finally, if she persists he may agree out loud, "All men are shits." He is now rejected by the woman and isolated from all other men as well. He is losing what should be most precious to him, his identity as a male person, because of a lack of boundaries. This is particularly true of the New Age man, or the man seeking "higher consciousness." He has not developed a good container for his soul much less a good container for two people. There's a leak somewhere. He feels it but doesn't want to look. He just hopes he can keep baling fast enough. Writing this angers me. It is no wonder women are so frustrated with men now days. She has to keep the container for both of them – that contains both their souls. She has every right to scream at him. He shows up but doesn't do any of the emotional work. Passivity and naiveté work hand in hand. The man reaches mid-life and is hollow inside. The woman has resigned herself to this ridiculous existence – or stepped out and is looking for a real man. The only thing that would hold her back is the unlikely prospect of finding one. The thing missing is for the man to stand up for his boundaries, know and say what he wants, set the limits of verbal abuse, and finally say "Enough." A woman may be channeling rage for dozens of dead generations of women. Taking on such rage is dangerous for a man and his son.

The naïve man often doesn't know that there is a being in him that wants to remain sick. Inside each man or woman there is a sick person and a well person: one needs to know which one is talking at any moment. But awareness of the sick being, and acknowledging how strong he is, is not part of the perception of the passive, naïve' man. He lacks "natural brutality" (James Hillman). The mother hawk pushes the younglings out of the nest one day; the father fox drives the cubs away in early October. A few harsh words of truth would have been helpful to the young boy. But we wait too long. Then a major wounding happens farther down the line. His timing is off. We notice that there will be a missing beat a second or so after he takes a blow, verbal or physical. He will go directly from the pain to an empathetic grasp of the reason why it came, skipping over the anger entirely. Misusing Jesus' words, he turns the other cheek.

Initiation means we look at our wounds and explore them. We learn who we are from them. We become emotionally competent. Robert Bly, talking about himself, relates: "In high school a girl might ask, 'Do you love me?' I couldn't answer. If I asked her the same question, she might reply, 'Well I respect you, and I admire you, and I'm fond of you, and I'm even interested in you, but I don't love you.' Apparently when she looked into her (heart), she saw a spectrum of affections, a whole procession of feelings, and she could easily tell them all apart. If I looked down into my heart, I saw nothing at all. I had then either to remain silent or fake it." Some women feel hurt when a man will not express his feelings, and they conclude that he is holding back or "telling them something" by such withholding; but it's more likely that when such a man asks a question of his heart, he gets no answer at all. Again, Robert Bly: "Now I can answer questions about my feelings and I can see people down there with different colored robes, walking around, and tell one from the other." This is all the result, he says of having stopped asking his parents for protection and having found men and women his own age to be his intimate partners in self-discovery. He feels "protected" by these people just as he did his parents as a child.

If we have led a "privileged" life and are at a loss for what to do, having finished college and being expected to be grown up, we can still initiate ourselves. We can take a job in the kitchen of a big hotel, take a job as a tradesman's apprentice, volunteer to maintain trails in a national park or any number of other "grounding" jobs that teach us our value as a man. As opposed to popular culture, our value does not relate to our salary but to our service, to our productivity. If we were lucky enough to grow up on a farm, we knew hard work from very early, and we could see the fruits of our labor. Most middle class boys now days don't understand their inherent value in this sense. They have never created anything. They have never made something happen. Life has been happening around them. So, when it comes to creating a life, they are clueless as to what that means or where to start. They look into their hearts and see nothing so they don't even know what they want. They can keep on living frivolously, or they can insist on something more. A suggested start, if one doesn't know what to do, is to get a job – any job – but preferably one with an "action equals outcome" framework. A dishwasher comes to mind. After a couple of years of this, if one has never been there before, a man develops a sense of having value. He acquires some sense of what he wants. He can then look into his heart and chose what to do next. And if with each experience he will just keep looking into his heart, he begins to see the many figures in different colored robes to which Bly refers, and he can begin to name them. He is now becoming a man in full. When he needs to be fierce he can be. When he needs to be gentle he can be. When he needs to say, "No", he can do so also. And he can embrace "yes" with an open heart. Women fight over such men.

Likewise, any man, regardless of his time and place in life, finds himself feeling empty and rudderless, not knowing what to do, he should "take an ordinary job." It is often not practical to become a dishwasher with a wife and three kids, but one can set about to connect with the essence of one's value by volunteering in a soup kitchen. Go on a regular basis. Get to know the people who come for a meal. Find out what makes you who you are through getting to know them. Or volunteer for maintenance in a nearby park, not once or twice but regularly for a couple of years. Get to know the walkers and the bench sitters. Let them see you with your work clothes on and a trash bag over your shoulder. For all they know you are working off community service. They may pull their children away from you at first. You are not wearing your professional clothes. It doesn't matter what they think. It is what you think and how you feel. Eventually, someone will say, "You are a little different than the average guy out here picking up trash." You say "Oh?" There is a certain delight in driving by the next day and seeing "your park" so clean and tidy. Sometimes you see something and have to stop to pick it up. How did that get there? The beer bottles tossed out of cars the night before will bother you. That used to be you. Now you "own" this park, this job. And it owns you. You have become valuable. You have seen a need and acted. Self love can not be created any other way for a man.

What I am saying is that the next step in initiation for men is down. Down is the "dark way" that Harvard or Yale does not prepare you for. One day a young man is in college, being fed and housed; the next he is homeless, walking the streets, looking for some way to get a meal and a bed – or he should be - rather than going home again. People know immediately when you are falling or have fallen: doormen turn their backs, waiters sneer, no one holds the subway car door for you. Old shame surfaces, except this time we are hopefully prepared to deal with it. We are not children any more. We remember that in the Bible Joseph's brothers put him down a deep dry well in the desert. A few days later they sell him to slave traders, who in turn take him still farther "down" into Egypt, where he descends into a dungeon after offending the commandant's wife. It is here, in this dungeon place, that he finds his gift. He finds it within himself and his communion with something larger than himself. He recognizes his gift of dream interpretation and much more, and his gifts are not just his own, they are born of the Divine.

Today these events are put off for decades, lifetimes, generations. Sometimes divorce, job loss or addiction, bring about this descent into one's soul work. A man may be deprived of not only his life and work, but his money, wife and children. Too often, a man, outwardly successful, living a sweet life, weekends in Tahoe, finds himself on his front lawn with a loaded shotgun in his mouth, about to pull the trigger. If he chooses not to pull the trigger he slinks back into the house having lost every shred of self respect. Carl Jung, when a person reported enthusiastically, "I have just been promoted!" was heard to respond, "I'm very sorry to hear that, but if we all stick together, I think we can get through it." On the other hand if a client arrived depressed and ashamed, saying, "I've just been fired", Jung would say, "Let's open a bottle of wine. This is wonderful news. Something good is about to happen." Whatever wounds we have received in childhood or adulthood can now be worked with. The wound is now a door. If we were abandoned by our parents, one way or the other, we are now associating with men and women who are chronically shamed. A man puts himself out where he can be shamed fifty times a day. But he can make a hero's exit through the wound. We need to have elders around to remind us how difficult it is to become a conscious father, a conscious husband, a conscious leader, a conscious man. "On the day I was born, God was sick." (Ce'sar Vallejo). The way down doesn't require poverty, homelessness, physical deprivation or dishwasher work necessarily, but it does require consciousness of the fall. Divorce, to most men, is like a discharge - as if one has been fired from one's task. The only way out of his former life is through the wound. Christ remarked, "You shall not get out until you have paid the last penny." Bly tells of a spiritual teacher driving back from a lecture on enlightenment, coming to a fork in the road. One way led to a motel where friends were and he knew there would be liquor and women. The other way led to the ascetic meditation center that he administered. He couldn't decide. The car went straight and crashed into a yellow brick wall advertizing THE JOKE SHOP. Which was the right way? Should he continue flying high on the ascetic life? Should be descend into the dangers of liaisons unknown? Was it really that straightforward? He was badly hurt. In the hospital, he got to think about the rest of his life and the meaning of what happened. He was profoundly changed. "Enlightenment" no longer seemed the goal. Something a little more earthy called to him.

Antonio Machado writes:

> *Mankind owns four things*
> *That are no good at sea –*
> *Rudder, anchor, oars,*
> *And the fear of going down.*

Sometimes we lose the boat in which we are floating through life. Sometimes life arranges a severe downfall if a man doesn't know to go down on his own. With depression, we refused to go down, so a hand reached up and pulled us down. With initiators gone from our culture, we do not receive instruction on how to go down on our own. Sufi groups like to begin their night-work not with a litany of what they have done wrong but a list of what they have failed to do in the last year. The emotion is not around sin, guilt, or shame but around what one has not done. The soul itself asks us to go down. If we become an alcoholic, the Twelve Steps take us down. The black side of the Great Mother in India is the Kali energy I referred to earlier. The flowers around her neck can change to skulls and back again in an instant, a real-life experience many boys and men can identify with. The only being who can stand up to her is Shiva. Only he contains the fierceness necessary to balance her dark side when it turns on him. Likewise, if we are to be free and fully male, we must also have at least this capacity. In old fables it was often depicted that the prince of the kingdom had to change places with the prince of the underworld for a period of time, before he could ascend the throne. If he refused or was not forced to do this, he would end up a fatally flawed "flying boy" who would lead his domain to rack and ruin. Practically, this sentence meant that he had to feel, next to him in bed all night, the body of the Black Darling, the Queen of the Underworld. Unless we face our programming from childhood and set off with determination and fierceness to find our own personal truth and the greater Truth, then we won't be who we want to be, who we can be. We have to sleep with the Black Darling. We don't have to make love to her, but we do have to find it in ourselves to face what we have been lead to believe, by our parents and our culture, and judge for ourselves what is true. We don't find freedom just by "looking" down into the dark, we have to replace for a time the childlike Eros we felt when our mother set a breast to our mouth, or our first marvelous girlfriend beckoned us to bed. These loves are all well and good but the descent is complete when both have been replaced by the boar-tusked, hog-bristled, big-mouthed, skull-necklaced, insanely high spirited energy of Black Kali. We have to go into our own personal swamp and face our own Marie Laveau, coming out scratched, bloody and a little crazy, but the only way we got out of there was to call out the Wild Man and be found an equal by the voodoo lady of our past. Brave young men often imagine when they look forward to meeting Black Kali that they can "kill" her. They imagine annihilation, total victory; but the stories make clear that such fantasies belong to the inexperienced, the uninitiated man. The only solution to the power of the witch is for the young man to develop energy as great as hers, as harsh, as wild, as shrewd, as clear in its desire. When a young man arrives at her house, proves himself to be up to her level of intensity, purpose and respect for the truth, she will sometimes say, "Okay, what do you want to know." Then and only then, we come home the king we were born to be, ready to rule over our kingdom with wisdom and benevolence. Young men in Viking times were allowed sometimes two or three years of "ashes" work. The Vikings lived in long houses, communal by nature, with perhaps thirty or forty beds lining the walls. Down the center of the hall was a pavement which acted as a fireplace. Ashes lay in long rows on either side of the fire. Of course, the young boys were often assigned to be the ash carriers. (Cinder-ella is the corresponding female story – usually one of the later children). In this system the first-born sons inherited everything and probably got to spend a lot of time with their fathers. It turns out that the younger boys sometimes would lie down in the area between the fire and the ash pile and stay there for two or three years. They undertook their own initiation of a different sort, eschewing cleanliness for an earthiness that gave them ritual value. The older men and women allowed it. If a young man now feels the need to drop out of school, there is no ritual for that. He is shamed or eventually may be imprisoned. In the 11th century, such a "cinder biter" named Starkad, remained in ashes for several years, until his foster father invited him to go on an expedition.

At that point he stood up, shaved, and dressed and became one of the best warriors on the expedition, and later become a distinguished poet as well. Perhaps the ashes suggest that before a boy can become a man, some infantile being in him must die. He instinctively knows this and "rolls" in the ashes until such an opportunity for emergence comes.

In the Pacific Islander tradition, boys between eight and twelve are taken away from their mothers by the old men guides, sometimes for days or weeks. These men cover the boy's faces with ashes and introduce them to their dead ancestors. Then finally, when they judge him ready, have him crawl through a tunnel, made of brush and branches. The old men are waiting on the other side to welcome the boy, only now he has a new name. The mothers pretend not to know him and have to be reintroduced. There then is a big celebration of the initiation, the mothers joining in.

Job covered himself in ashes to signify the old, comfortable Job was dead. He was no longer a "flying boy" of wealth and privilege. It turns out that it was not enough to follow the rules that make us feel righteous - giving us the "favor" of God. He was pulled down, perhaps as an example, or as an allegory for us all. "Now they mock me, men younger than I, whose fathers I would have disdained to put with my sheep dogs." (Job 30:1) He rails against the Lord's unfairness and whines and argues with all those who come to him. The Lord finally answers: "Who is this that darkens my counsel with words without knowledge? Brace yourself like a man; I will question you, and you shall answer me. Where were you when I laid the earth's foundation? Tell me, if you understand. Who marked off its dimensions? Surely you know! Who stretched a measuring line across it? Who shut up the sea behind doors when it burst forth from the womb, when I made the clouds its garment and wrapped it in thick darkness, when I fixed limits for it and set its doors and bars in place, when I said, 'This far you may come and no farther, here is where your proud waves halt'. Have you given orders to the morning, or shown the dawn it's place, that it might take the earth by the edges and shake the wicked out of it?... Do you send the lightning bolts on their way? Do they report to you, "Here we are. Who endowed the heart with wisdom?" (Job 38, 1-36)

Job tries to answer out of pride, defiance and self-pity. We are given no clues about Job's early life but apparently he was badly in need of a male presence. He finally submits. "My ears have heard you but now my eyes have seen you. Therefore I despise myself and repent in dust and ashes." For some reason this epic story has never been lifted up as one of the greatest stories of all time of belated initiation into the Truth. It is then recorded; "The Lord blessed the latter part of Job's life more than the first... Nowhere in all the land was there found women as beautiful as Job's daughters, and their father granted them an inheritance along with their brothers." (Job, 42, 12-15). He became an enlightened man through this ordeal. "After this, Job lived a hundred and forty years; he saw his children and their children to the fourth generation. And he died old and full of years." A true elder – what a blessing he must have been to his extended family. Being pulled down brought him out of his moral superiority into true wisdom and service.

Now we live in Disneyland, where there is no sign of trash, much less ashes. It is a young man's dream that by the time he is thirty-five he will have a Nobel Prize, be CEO of a Fortune 500 company and be married to Miss America. He will finally get out of this hick town and live in Paris. By the time he is forty-five, all these dreams are ashes. As Jung would say, "This is wonderful news. Something good is about to happen." His inner stove is beginning to produce ashes as well. He has been burning the candle at both ends but notices that his stove no longer takes such big chunks of "wood" anymore. He opens the stove door and ashes fall out on the floor. It is time to find a small black shovel and get down on his knees and begin the ashes work.

Men often find around this time that all their relationships are turning to ashes. Some habitual error we keep making, born of our unacknowledged infantile perceptions, produces still more heat. Men become afraid to commit to a relationship because it is too painful. Sometimes we just have to sit down by the fire, smear soot on our faces and hope that the Wild Man finds us.

Franklin Roosevelt found his ashes in his polio; Solzhenitsyn in the Gulag, Nelson Mandela in his prison. After Achilles killed Hector, his father, Priam, longed to get Hector's body back to Troy for a proper burial. Priam, with the help of Hermes, was guided at night; stealthily through the enemy lines of the Greeks, into the heart of the camp to retrieve the body. So we have to slip at night "past the lines" to find the corpse – to return it to ashes. It requires cunning and stealth. It requires the help of a God. Of course, Zeus burned the Titans to ashes. Human beings were born of those ashes. In the movie, *Casualties of War*, an actual incident in the Vietnam War is recounted where four men in a platoon of five capture, then rape, then finally kill a Vietnamese woman. None of the four is properly a man at all, but they are all brutal boys, stuck in some stage before descent and ashes work would have taught them to see the women as another human being. The fifth man refuses to take part in the rape, tries to save the woman's life and later reports the incident at risk of his own life. He is threatened with being raped himself by these men. As we see, the brutal, dehumanizing male is a result of not having been properly instructed, initiated and welcomed into manhood by his elders. The man who sees the woman as another human being, as they really are, male or female, is the man who could save us all from ourselves. May he rise up again and be welcomed. He may be crucified but he is the only hope we have.

As I have said, many initiation rites still exist today in "more primitive" societies. The old men come with spears to get the boys and the mothers feign resistance. The boys are afraid and cry out "Momma, save me!" to no avail. Afterwards the women get to together for coffee and say things like, "How did I do? Did I look fierce enough in trying to hold onto my son?" "You were great." These "gender issues" as we call them, are well understood by these societies as necessary to have real men doing their part in running the tribe. Otherwise they end up with a bunch of shiftless, irresponsible "tomcats" so evident in some the matriarchal ghetto cultures until recently. The women reluctantly have to take over all the adult responsibilities, while these fatherless men live as perpetual adolescents. The relevant sentence accepted in the initiation rites of so-called primitive cultures is, "A boy cannot change into a man without the active intervention of the older men." A girl changes into a woman, given her obvious bodily developments, with the attendant explanations and context supplied by the older women. The women celebrate these things among themselves with rituals and ceremonies. Childbirth is the ultimate female initiator.

But a break from the mother is only a break and it doesn't imply any internal movement inside the boy. With most of us, it is still happening, but without some effort on an elder's part, it may have never been started. A man must move from his mother's house to his father's house. Shakespeare's Hamlet is a brilliant description of the difficulty of the move. Hamlet is a "prince" in every sense; brilliant, educated and handsome. But he has never done any dirty work. He struggles to move into his full manhood. Ophelia dies for lack of being met halfway by a decisive, determined man. The feminine suffers from the lack of expression of a true masculine presence. His father, the dead king, comes to him as a ghost to urge him on – "Shudder over my death, look at the ashes of my kingship, give up your studious life." Hamlet has no other elder male in his life to help him. His mother's house is too comfortable. His father has to come back again and again to keep things moving. Hamlet eventually, reluctantly, tortuously manages to outwit those who would take advantage of his naiveté. Inside, he knows what he has to do. In the end, Hamlet finally arrives at his father's house, his own mother dies, he draws his sword and kills his father's murderer. Of course, he also ends up getting killed himself. Most people seemed trapped in the "tragedy" of this moment. But Hamlet stepped into his manhood, always fraught with danger, at that moment. He dies after saying, "Things standing thus unknown, shall live behind me! If thou didst ever hold me in thy heart, absent thee from felicity awhile. And in this harsh world draw thy breath in pain, and tell my story." - The story of a boy, a prince, becoming a king, a man, if only for a moment. (Act V, Scene II, 353-357)

A man's effort to move to the father's house takes a long time. It is difficult and each man has to do it for himself. For Hamlet it meant giving up the immortality or the safe life promised to the faithful mother's son, and accepting the risk of death always imminent in the father's realm. Joseph Campbell, in *Occidental Mythology*, noted that he observed a certain scene over and over on numerous Babylonian seals. We see a male figure standing, and nearby we see a female figure, probably a goddess or the goddess's priestess, and we see a third figure, a large snake. We have to remember that in the ancient world, the snake was not considered evil, but a holy animal. Here, Campbell speculated that the snake represented the masculine. It is possible that such a seal was an object for men to meditate on, in a culture ruled by the Great Mother. The snake was the way to escape from the Great Mother's, and his own mother's field. He is no longer a "flying boy" identifying with the bird, but now begins his earthy, dirty, ashes work, crawling on the ground like a snake. But he is also able to climb trees to get the longer perspective and swim in the deep waters of the soul successfully. Like a snake, he sheds his old skin and becomes a new man.

The Old Testament was being formulated in the minds of the

ancients at about the same time as the Babylonian myths. Although it has been twisted almost beyond recognition, we see "The Fall of Man" here. Eve eats of the fruit first and then hands it to Adam, who does what she says. The snake may not have been so evil after all. The age of innocence is over. "Your eyes will be opened", says the snake. (Gen, 3). True enough. God says, "You will crawl on your belly and you will eat dust…" in response to finding out that Adam is still obeying a woman. But this "initiation" is into an opportunity for full divinity for both man and woman. Adam and Eve are no longer "flying boys and girls", with everything handed to them on a silver platter. They are now in partnership with God in the creation of humanity. It may not always be fun, but it's real.

THE LOSS OF COMBATIVE DIALOGUE

In the old school of education, from Socrates on down, teachers used to aggressively question the students. One learned to survive and thrive in these sessions. Men gained self-esteem through this process. Even in the old Tibetan monasteries of the twelfth and thirteenth centuries, young Buddhist novices would stand against the walls, lining the corridor, while the teacher walked between them, shouting questions and expecting shouted answers in return.

In my own training it was de' rigueur to be asked questions, directed to an individual in a group, as one make rounds with the professor. The student was on the spot in front of his peers. The worst was standing in an operating room, "scrubbed in" as the third assistant to the professor performing the procedure, and being grilled continuously as a running dialogue, while one's arm was numb to the shoulder from holding a retractor for hours on end. "What muscle is this?" "What does it do?" "What vein is this?" "What would happen if I clamped it?" One learned to think on one's feet, under pressure, in front of others. One learned to ask questions in return, with just the right amount of assertiveness – engaging the professor in a dialogue that demonstrated one's readiness for one's own practice. This behavior by professors, of course wouldn't be tolerated today. I have already talked about the down side of the strictly masculine teaching style of the past. Yet something has been lost as well. When fierce debate is no longer considered appropriate, boys don't learn how to defend themselves in such circumstances.

Often now, I see young men, when confronted with aggression of some sort, try to placate the aggressor or simply turn away. These naïve men are at a disadvantage if they have not learned to face aggression with assertiveness. In the cultivation of their feminine side they have denied their masculine side.

The warrior ideals have a place in business as well. Since the time of the shoguns, the Japanese have studied the self-sacrificial acts the warrior ideal requires. That study seems to have strengthened the responsibility or duty they accept toward their employees or employer. In the United States, the company owners of the nineteenth century had so little sense of duty that the unions had to step in to protect the workers. These days the chief executives in America move from company to company lightly, vote themselves bonuses just before bankruptcy, and sell out the retirement fund. These men are certainly not looking out for the greater good. It is odd how infrequently the taxpayers gather with their swords drawn against these outrages, or against savings and loan greediness, or against the presidential campaigner's refusal to debate the issues. Many men are literally or figuratively unable to extend their arm in combat or their tempered words in debate. Given a sword, symbolic or not, men of today would often throw it down or break it, in fear of disapproval, or believing such action to be appropriate revulsion of masculine behavior. Thus our society is taken advantage of by the new robber barons. The Tibetans refer to such a sharp interior sword as "The Vajra Sword." Without it, they say, no spiritual life is possible – and no adult life.

We may also need such a sword to cut us apart from our own self-pity. Victimhood may have been in attentively joined to us when we were children. The Greeks admired a Pelasgean creation myth in which "once upon a time" an egg floated on the ocean. Then a sword approached, cutting the egg in two. Inside the egg was Eros, freed by the slashing sword. If the egg had remained intact, there would have been no Eros in the world. No sword, no Eros. The parent's love for the child, the man's love for a woman, the woman's love for a man, the bees' love for the hive, the worshipper's love for God – none of that comes into being without the action of the Divine Sword. They called this Divine Cutter, Logos.

BEYOND THE WARRIOR

So, what must we do to become men among men? I have already alluded to the fact that we must get in touch with our fierceness. The wounds we have all received need to be gone into and understood. Up to one hundred years ago, we had many men to teach us the rhythm of masculinity. Our grandfather told stories, our uncle told us about women and we got to see our father at work every day. We got to work beside them.

Now we are suspicious of older men. They are to be made fun of. We have been taught to trust the feminine point of view (through no fault of our mothers). The void of masculine validation has to be filled with something. We learn to trust the feminine. We assume a woman knows more about what to do then we do. When we are scolded by women, we assume it is for our "own good." In order to be healthy, we need to get in touch with our anger.

It is not appropriate to rise up in anger at every remark. First we have to identify those images taught to us in childhood about masculinity. After we have "gone down" and come to know those voices, to know ourselves and our components, we can begin to parse out what is real and appropriate and what is not. A woman cannot know what is right for us. She can be wise and set us on a course, but she can not sit with us and explain our urges. We need to cultivate the warrior. The warrior draws his sword and separates the wheat from the chaff. The warrior draws his sword to defend "the king." The king is our sense of self worth, our right to have the feeling we are having. The warrior defends us, our inner king. This warrior does not cross the boundary to abuse other people. This warrior is there to define and defend our boundary. He is loyal above all, to his king (his inner essence). He is tenacious in his pursuit of his hero's goal. He never gives up. Along with loyalty, justice is his highest value. A child concludes that if it has no sovereignty, it must be worthless. Shame is the name we give to the sense that we are unworthy and inadequate as human beings. Crossing our boundary should make us angry. If it doesn't, we are ashamed of ourselves. We remind ourselves of our fathers. We have been taught this by our culture. It is no wonder that such a child, when a teenager, looks for protection, reassurance. His only resource may be a girl or a gang. Over and over he says, "I am a victim" and he is. This very identification with victimhood keeps him vulnerable to still more invasions and degradations. Unless the warrior arises to defend the house of the soul, he lives in ongoing grief.

The Warrior is the transition to the King. In archetypal mythology, the warrior goes out in service of the king. He takes a hero's journey. If he does not die during his quest, like Hamlet and Jesus, he returns with great riches and assumes the sovereign throne. The king is not about domination and power. He is about service to the greater good. Remember, he may be chosen by the women, but always accepts the role reluctantly but in understanding of his duty to the people he serves. Inside of every boy and girl is a king or a queen. The world would squash these parts of us. Unless we can evoke the energy of the warrior, we will not assume the role of ruler of our lives.

Men have been taught to quash the warrior in today's world. But in men, at least, it is hard-wired. The question is will we honor that part of us. The alternative is to spend a tremendous amount of energy suppressing it. The warrior's area of expertise is the battlefield. The war that takes place there can be physical war, psychological war or spiritual war. If the king he serves is corrupt, like Ollie North, or there is no king at all but he is serving greed and power, then he is a mercenary, not a warrior. In mythology, when a warrior, is elevated above a king, he ends up destroying the empire. He needs to battle the demons of his own soul first, before he can become wise. A warrior in service, however, to the True King – that is to a transcendent cause – does well. His body becomes a hardworking servant, which he requires to endure cold, heat, pain, wounds, scarring, hunger, lack of sleep, hardship of all kinds. The person in touch with the warrior can work long hours, ignore fatigue, finish the Ph.D. and all the footnotes, write under a single dangling light bulb for years, clean up the shit and filth endlessly like Saint Francis or Mother Teresa, endure contempt, disdain and exile. The comfort-loving baby becomes subservient to the determined, resilient man and an adult warrior inhabits the body. Women today have assumed this role. They are equally entitled to this energy. Sadly, men are no longer meeting them half way.

Norse and Celtic literature and Ernest Hemingway in *The Old Man and the Sea* describe the warriors who went "too far". They were introduced to their own inner limitations and had to be carefully reintegrated into the human community. They taught us wisdom through their wound. Now we let our warriors go berserk and then simply discharge them to the streets. A man who cannot defend his own space cannot defend women and children. The drug lords prey primarily for recruits on kingless, warriorless boys.

In the male mythological story, *Iron John*, the country is swept up into war. The King gathered his forces but is seriously in doubt of his ability to defend the kingdom. The "cinder boy" tells the king that he is quite grown now and is ready to go to battle in defense of the kingdom, if they will only give him a horse. The other men laugh and declare: "When we've gone, you go look in the stable. We will have certainly left a horse behind." When they have gone, he goes into the barn and finds a horse, lame in one leg. He climbs on and rides off toward the battle. He calls on his resource, Iron John, his Wild Man, to assist him. "What do you want", says Iron John. "I want a strong war-horse because I intend to go to war." The Wild Man then summons a stable boy leading out a war-horse that blows air through its nostrils and is not easy to handle. Running along behind is a large band on warriors, all clad in iron from head to foot. The boy mounts the new horse and rides out at the head of these warriors. By the time he reaches the battlefield, most of the King's men are dead. The boy and his iron band ride in at full speed like a hurricane and strike down every one that opposes the kingdom. The enemy turns to flee, but the boy keeps after them and pursues them to the last man.

The invasion here is more than a distraction or an annoyance. The story says that the King is losing the battle. Apparently the center of the psyche cannot protect its own territory. If the King is actually losing the battle, it is time for the warrior in us to learn how to fight. We notice that the warrior pursues the battle to the end, unlike Saul who therefore loses his kingship. No halfway measures are appropriate. No therapy for the invader. If there is no decisive move, the battle will be lost. In many stories, in the spring, a sprouting of nourishing grain is seen to occur from the fallen bodies of the invaders. In ritual space, we know this to be true. It is only after we have ridden the "lame" horse into battle, the fourth leg having been shamed, and called out our Wild man to enable our stead, that we can overcome the invaders that defile our soul. When we were tiny, our horse had all four legs and it lived joyfully in whatever it could gallop to. By the time a child is twelve, one of the legs is crippled by shame, whether we grew up in a dysfunctional household or not. None of us know how to heal our horse of such shame. We have to bring it to an older man. Or we have to invoke our own Wild Man. We take the old nag out of the barn where the older boys have left it. We rise up in recognition of our woundedness. Somehow this empowers our stead. We ride off, suddenly the commander of an army. If we are smart we pursue the foes to the last man. However, this event does not do away with our early shaming; that cannot be done away with. But we can keep it "in front of us" as an awareness of our woundedness. Now we have a choice whether to act out of that woundedness or out of our new found power to set boundaries and defend them. And we can work to prevent further shaming. We can find our connection to that earlier four-legged horse.

We can again become the prince, who like Siddhartha, sought ignominy outside the castle, and found his life, which he then sought to give to others.

When a man has become aware of his woundedness and dealt with it through fiercely rising up and cutting free of the invisible fetters of his childish perceptions, he is no longer controlled by them. When a man can look back into his past, doing so without regret and instead seeing only lessons that brought him to his current strength and wisdom, he embraces the fullness of who he can become. He can move forward into his life's future. Seeing his own divinity, he begins to recognize the divinity in all men and women. He can begin to see his body and his mind as a temple to be appreciated and defended. Although the old wounds will never disappear, they will be scarred over, and he can now begin to use them to empower him. Having become a warrior in order to cut away the fetters, he can now move on to become the king of his own life. He can't get stuck in perpetual warriorhood, lest he become a General Patton, a Karl Marx or a Nietzsche. On the other hand, he can not think that he has "overcome" his woundedness. It is the ability to look occasionally at the "scars" that makes him a great king. No scars, no kingdom.

Many men say they simply don't know anymore what a man is supposed to be – what the word "man" means. But when another man riskily names some qualities that he sees as masculine, we can judge for ourselves how far we are from that spot, and he can also. It is in honest dialogue, even in our emotional ignorance, that we have hope of becoming grown up and of service to others. We must remember the battles and be willing to return to them if necessary, albeit reluctantly.

Our scars remind us of our wounds in battle and keep us "grounded" in the reality of who we are. It is only such a person who can rule his life wisely. Jacob, of the Bible, once so clever he could outwit his brother, and having strength without peer, wrestles with God and finally receives a wound, limping the rest of his life in remembrance. He may have "gone out too far" in testing his limits, which he thought were without bounds, but in the process is "blessed" with a wound that transforms him into the man who is renamed Israel. He is no longer "the golden boy." He carries his woundedness, transforming his ordeal into wisdom. He ascends to the leadership of his people. Literature is replete with such stories, attesting to the importance of finding our woundedness and moving on despite it. Saint Paul reluctantly referred to his "thorn in the flesh." We cannot move on into full adult partnerships, responsibilities and leadership without having become comfortable with who we are and from where we come. Even if we are forty or sixty, we must do this work if we are to reclaim our rightful kingship of our own lives. A mature man can be recognized by his awareness of his own woundedness but his unwillingness to let it deter him from his steadfastness.

> *"You've seen a herd of goats*
> *going down to the water.*
> *The lame and dreamy goat*
> *brings up the rear.*
> *There are worried faces about that one,*
> *But ah, now they're laughing, because look,*
> *as they return,*
> *That goat is the leader!*
> *There are many different kinds of knowing.*
> *The lame goat's kind is a branch*
> *that traces back to the roots of Presence.*
> *Learn from the lame goat,*
> *and lead the herd Home."*
>
> —Rumi, Persian poet

Native Americans have a tradition about scars. Lame Deer recalls in his autobiography, "When you die, you meet the Old Hag, and she eats your scars. If you have no scars, she will eat your eyeballs, and you will be blind in the next world." No scars, no hope for vision. We know from multiple ancient sources that a shaman must be a wounded man. Through his wound he has become "double-hearted" - his physical heart - and the wound that beats with compassion.

A Concord woman recorded a description of Emerson, Hawthorne and Thoreau ice skating. Emerson leaned constantly forward into the wind. Hawthorne skated like an immensely calm statue. Thoreau gave little leaps and pirouettes constantly. Having gone deep, one is filled with joy and freedom. The Wild Man doesn't come to full life through being "natural", going with the flow, smoking weed, drinking beer, reading nothing and being generally groovy. It comes with recognition and integration of our wounds – going deep.

> *"I am content to follow to its source*
> *Every event in action or in thought;*
> *Measure the lot; forgive myself the lot!*
> *When such as I cast out remorse*
> *So great a sweetness flows into the breast*
> *We must laugh and we must sing,*
> *We are blest by everything,*
> *Everything we look upon is blessed."*
>
> —*A Dialogue of Self and Soul*, W.B. Yeats

It is now that a man is ready to step out of being a warrior. It is now that he is ready to rule his life. It is now that he is ready to make decisions that last a lifetime. It is now that the masculine and feminine can come together in true partnership.

CHAPTER ELEVEN:

INVEST IN A PARTNER

If we, as men, are fortunate enough to arrive at awareness of the need to find out who we are emotionally and some of the "whys", by say, forty-five years old, then we are right on schedule. We begin to know the "buttons" that produce emotional responses from us and can take responsibility for access to those "buttons." We have gone deep and know what makes us tick. We have begun to accept ourselves and are able to make choices in the expression of the various forces jockeying for expression inside us. We are now ready to step into a real partnership with another person, having taken responsibility for ourselves. Most of us probably already have or have had a significant relationship or two by now. We can turn outside of ourselves and begin to cultivate that relationship that will be an investment, drawing interest, for the rest of our lives.

We have some control over ourselves because we have gone deep and can see the components of which we are made. We have the ability to make choices. It is important for a man to make choices, establish boundaries, and pay the price of the labor that follows his choosing – one queen, one goddess. Too often now we hear, "I want it all," attempting to vindicate greediness and love of being unlimited. Choosing our one person of desire and sticking with that person is the mark of a mature warrior becoming a king. This is the second important piece of the foundation of mature masculinity. Fidelity is an important part of growing up and gaining second adulthood. It is the price we pay for our significant other that appreciates her value.

The passion in our nature urges a human being to choose "the one precious thing" and urges him to pay for it through poverty, conflict, deprivation, labor and the endurance of the painful awareness of other roads not taken.

Most of us already have a long-standing relationship with a lot of history. Out of ignorance, we have assumed that the relationship is mutually satisfying. Often we are focused elsewhere– on our careers, our many forms of "hunting", while we leave the "nesting" and gathering to our partner. Hopefully, a commitment has developed that will provide a spring board for true partnership once we realize our relationship can be so much more than it has been. Unfortunately, we often wait for a crisis before we think about such investments at home. The time to start investing in our primary partner is before we need it! It is like the miracle of compound interest. It does not do much good to start putting money in the company's 401K when you hit fifty. The small amounts put in at twenty-five, thirty and thirty-five pay off big later on - likewise with our primary relationship. Too often we waste these years because we are so full of ourselves and think the way we are now (at twenty-five), in all our glory, will go on forever. We are too busy warrioring to pay attention to our inner being or the inner workings of our significant other.

Why is it important to cultivate a long-term, committed relationship? We need another person in order to become who we will need to become to cope successfully with today's world, with its extended longevity. We need another person to explore an emotional life with and to enjoy it when we find it. We will need such a relationship when we reach mid-life and we begin to slow down physically. After thirty-five, when our testosterone begins declining, we don't notice anything at first but after about forty-five we will. It helps to have a long-term partner to go through this transition with us. If we have not cultivated our primary relationship, we may not have the empathy and understanding we need. Women like men to show their vulnerability and we will learn vulnerability whether we like it or not. Women like men to talk about their fears, hopes and desires – and we have recently developed some awareness of what our inner terrain looks like. This time of life, then, can be the beginning of an extended deepening of our relationship with our spouse that lays a foundation of strength on which we can build a useful second adulthood – or if her rage has been building up for decades, it can be a time of painful sorting out and decision making. Either way, we are on a path toward authenticity and truth.

It is often helpful to find a group of men with whom to "test drive" our deep emotional work, before we risk sharing some of our fears and vulnerabilities with a woman. Sometimes our significant other has truly become our best and trusted friend and she is the sounding board that we need. One has to realize however, because of our different ways of thinking and perceiving, a woman may not understand where we are coming from, whereas a man may immediately identify. In fact, we need both to occur. We need to find a group of intimate male friends with whom to discuss where we go from here at mid-life. We need to form an intimate group of men to mentor younger men in "going deep" and the cultivation of their primary relationship. In addition, we need to come up with a set of "ground rules" with which to begin to explore a deeper emotional relationship with our sex partner.

GROUND RULES

The single most important rule to use in all encounters with the opposite sex, not involving simple factual exchange, is to "honor" what they say. That means that we must believe that what they say is true for them. We may not understand why, but now that we know our brains operate and value things differently, we can accept the fact that what they are saying is a valid attempt to communicate what is important for them. Likewise, we need to insist that what we are saying is true for us, and also needs to be respected. How else are we to find out what we really believe and want unless we say it out loud and "try it on for size". It is a difficult but rewarding discipline, to "listen carefully" to what the other person is saying and rather than rebutting it, say, "I understand that is how you feel" or "I understand that is what you want" and mean it without "ifs", "ands" or "buts." We need to tell the truth as best that we know it and assume the other is doing so too. Out of this we develop mutual respect and a vision of the terrain on which we stand. It will lead to a common path or compromise with which we can both live joyfully, out of mutual trust that the other will keep their end of the bargain.

If we must fight, fight fairly. Conscious fighting involves playing by a set of agreed upon rules. Stick to the subject at hand. Don't bring in past events to bolster one's argument. Don't pull out any "weapons" that you have not agreed upon beforehand. Say what is true for you and listen and accept the other as true for them. Instead of tearing down their argument, bolster your own. Neither party labels the other as "the problem." Neither holds the other solely responsible for the issue. Attacking the other person in a stage of "being possessed" by the shamed child in yourself is not going to do anything but injure your partner and create remorse in yourself. However, it is inevitable that these things will happen. A man or a woman will start raising his or her voice in a way that feels threatening or make threatening gestures, such as a man standing up. A man or a woman may begin to label what the other says as "stupid" or "childish", shaming them and inducing predictable child-based rage in the other. When these things happen, the other partner must say, "That is not OK," and name the behavior. The partner must then cease the behavior and return to "conscious" fighting or call a "time out" in which to regain composure, after which the origin of his or her behavior may need to be discussed before going on with the original topic. If one partner insists on repeatedly losing control of "fairness", the other simply says, "I will not allow myself to be talked to that way, and I am leaving." Respect must be demanded by both partners.

As men, we may be behind in our emotional clarity but in order to find it securely, we need to accept the fact that the "warrior" will need to come out - to right supposed wrongs and defend newly-developed boundaries. Some of the things that will come out will have nothing to do with the partner to whom we are speaking. That may only become obvious in the light of having said it. Trust your partner. Apologize when appropriate. Be brave. Take risks. Fight fair. Remember, a warrior is disciplined. The intimacy and love that results will be a ten-fold reward.

We now have a foundation in understanding how men's and women's brains work. We know that the ways in which men and women have evolved cause different behavior and different perceptions. We know that we have different ways of saying, "I love you." Men are more likely to volunteer to do the dishes than actually verbally express their affection because that feels more meaningful to them. Words are "cheap" compared to actions for most men. We know that most women would rather have a man stay seated at the dinner table and discuss the day's happenings face to face with full emotional embellishment and to have the favor returned by their partner, than jumping up to do the dishes. We know that men tend to feel close to someone when they are working or playing side by side. We know that women feel close by talking to someone they care about and sharing their most intimate feelings. We know that many men struggle to access and name how they feel. We know that men often don't naturally express those feelings and that when they do, they may simply be trying to please their significant other. We know that men are more likely to need "process" time before they can respond meaningfully. We know that most women can launch into a meaningful conversation about what's going on at the drop of a hat. We know that men tend to value and seek a solution rather than wallow in the feeling, which is uncomfortable for them. We know that men tend to respond to difficulty by "clamming up", while women want to talk about it. Finally, we know that when a man becomes emotional, he perceives it as being "out of control" and to be avoided at all costs. When a woman does so, she is just "having an emotion" and it may not threaten her. In short, we realize now how different we are. The amount of DNA on the Y chromosome that males and females don't share, is greater than the DNA difference between us and chimpanzees! Of course, the content of that DNA makes much more profound differences evident, but the fact does accentuate just how much variation there is between the genders. Why would our brains as well as our bodies to be so different? In a word – it is complementarity.

COMPLEMENTARITY

The concept of complementarity has been around for a long time. The famous Danish physicist Neils Bohr developed it to explain observations in quantum physics. Bohr concluded that profound opposites, when taken together, constitute a complete description of a total reality. In this case, for a species, both genders have to be kept in mind to understand the total reality.

For our purposes, the total reality of the s/he brain is contained in the genotype of the species and the gender differences expressed are the complementary aspects of that reality. Not all characteristics of the sex-specific female brain apply to all females and vice versa. Complementarity requires us to describe any individual human brain is terms of the total reality of the s/he brain. Overlap between male and female brains is implicit, but the full survival-enhancing expression of the divine-directed characteristics and talents of a species, can only be found when males and females work together. The logic of Aristotle, on which Western society is based, tells us that when the world is divided into differences, that the two different sides, although they may be equal, cannot be the same. To treat them so is to guarantee that at least one side, if not both, will result in unequal benefit. So how do we respond to things that are different but equal? We respond by recognizing and responding to them as different. It is only in this recognition and acceptance that the benefit of the differences can be enjoyed. Paid maternity leave, adequate child care and fair and equitable treatment of mothers in divorce and custody hearings are not optional – they are inalienable rights. This new standard, however, would also recognize the fact that the total reality includes sex-specific bodies and brains. What is best for the children, may not result in "same" treatment of the parents.

It has become apparent that men and women were born to complement one another. This puts a whole different perspective on the "gender wars." Embracing and cultivating our differences is the key to our success as a species. Denying limits us all. One's significant other of the opposite gender is someone to be explored and enjoyed as an important counterpart in co-creation. If the "male" way is linear and the "woman's" way is "lateral" thinking, how can we come to the full truth without both perspectives? One projects ahead on a linear path, the next step and the consequences. The other takes into consideration the emotional content of the present and past and their implications in any decision in the present moment. Where one's intuitive leap facilitates the other's process, the other's gifts iron out the details or flesh out the implications. A man or a woman, while they may be competent as individuals, are not all they can be without the other. First we must understand this. Secondly, we must learn to appreciate the differences that balance us as good. Finally, we must pursue a relationship with "the other" that recognizes these facts and encourages the utilization of these differences to our advantage and enjoyment. Just like in sexual intercourse, men and women are made to fit together, and neither can hope to have an enjoyable experience of life without the other. We are "individuals" by virtue of our genes and experience. We are "persons" by virtue of our relationships.

CHAPTER TWELVE:

FINDING A PURPOSE GREATER THAN OURSELVES

"Buddha left a road map. Jesus left a road map. Krishna left a road map. Rand McNally left a road map. But you still have to travel the road yourself."

—*Stephen Levine*

The goal of this book is this: To adopt responsible self-acceptance which will lead to coaching ourselves as men through self-awareness and self-realization, resulting in a mature manhood of service to the larger good. To reach this goal, however, we not only have to understand ourselves but we need to move on from our initial way of being, that frame of reference. Our body and brain was designed to be used for a lifespan roughly half the length of our current one. It was based on a physical model that terminates us at the end of our period of peak physical ability as a hunter. Once we started to decline, if we had survived that long at all, we were a threat to no longer be capable of producing more than we used, or supporting the children we might produce. We had "used up" our primary value to the tribe and came to face our mortality. The natural order managed this transition just fine. In this primitive setting, declining physical prowess took care of eliminating itself.

That is not the case now. The hard-driving, aggressive, focused male style that so facilitated the hunter, if it is coupled with a new awareness of our origin, may still serve for the first half of our lives. However, a new, conscious paradigm needs to be developed for the extension of our lives, for the years beyond which the design was intended. To this end, it is incumbent upon men to reach for and find a new style of living for later life - "a second adulthood." This second adulthood can be characterized by not only self-knowledge and self-acceptance but by a refocusing on finding a new passion in life. This new passion, this new meaning-creation, traditionally, involved mentoring and wisdom leadership. Before men and boys became separated by industrial society, this was the paradigm that permeated our culture. This transition to second adulthood is often a radical transformation from our youthful way of being and living.

The pathways of this transition are many and individual but follow archetypal patterns. This hero's journey is not only for ourselves. It is for all of society, so sorely lacking in the male modeling of what an elder man is and does. Instead of men seeking to forever act like we are young, we can seek to pull the younger generation into responsible living, working and loving. Elder men can again be looked up to with aspiration by the young, through acting responsibly and demanding respect. We can seek to lead middle age men into a second adulthood that actually seems desirable –not something from which to run. We can support one another in eldership. Follow me as I elucidate what this eldership might look like.

We can transform the negative sense of a "mid-life" crisis" into a "mid-life opportunity". Men need a plan for the second half of life – a life for which men were not prepared by evolution. It can be quite a shock. It can result in primitive behavior. Instead, let's lay out a plan for this transition that honors us and our partners. Women can be our allies in this process. Other men can be of great value.

This new pathway can include a passion for renewing our role in society. Our culture is sorely in need of elders. Let's consider how the symptoms of the breakdown of the health of our society are largely due to the breakdown of male eldership. The overwhelming prison population, largely young men, the school shootings occurring again and again in middle class neighborhoods, teenage sexual activity at an all time high and involving younger and younger children, are a few of the symptoms. Where are the fathers, the "Dutch uncles", the older brothers? In short, where are the men?

So, the goal of second adulthood for men is not just to save ourselves. It is a response to a floundering society as much as it is a response to the struggle we find inside ourselves – the struggle to find meaning after midlife. We can therefore, kill two birds with one stone. We can recreate meaning and purpose in the lives of men after midlife while recreating the role of the elder male in society. These are the men of wisdom who demand respect. These are the men that draw young men into manhood and keep them in line. They honor the budding sexuality of young women. They respect each other, women and the earth.

Men growing into second adulthood and the evolving solutions to many of American society's problems go hand in hand. Let us explore, explain, and discover a solution. Let us call one another to responsibility. Let us come down squarely on the side of the intention of giving new life to men, and all beings, and the planet. Let us invite men to take up the challenge of stepping into a second adulthood – the "next" life that will be characterized by intentional living, intentional service and intentional transformation.

We no longer know when we have reached the stage of eldership because there is no right of passage. Maybe we need to create one. No matter what "symptom", what nagging feeling, or what event, brings us to the process of reaching for second adulthood, the important thing is the message. It is time. Something is happening to us. The passage to the second half of life is starting. If you feel you are in a state of denial, do not assume it is inappropriate. Resistance may be a part of your way of preparing yourself. There is only one way out and that is through. Without confusion no clarity can emerge. Confusion is the mother of change. Listen to your body. It is inviting the transition. When our bodies fail to work, we should treat them like honored messengers, bringing important news.

Again, from *The Accidental Tourist*: Macon says of Muriel, his new love at midlife, "She gave me another chance to decide who I am."

If we focus on ourselves as we get older and continue to deteriorate, mentally and physically, one is destined to become terminally depressed. If, on the other hand, one focuses on others, we see that we still can make a difference, that we still have effect. We can still see our impact on outcomes. We can still feel power. Whether it's helping a grandchild with their homework, taking a call from a young person at college, seeking advice and afraid to tell his parents, or rallying for your favorite political cause, it's all about being available to share our experience with others. We need to make it our goal every day – like brushing our teeth – to find that passion. The search process for the path of passionate second adulthood is what keeps hope alive.

Greek Mythology tells the story of Chiron, the archetypal wounded healer. Chiron was a master healer and teacher, who had been severely wounded early in life, by his mother's rejection. All the great Greek heroes were brought to Chiron for training as children. He taught them, not only the art of healing but also warrior-ship, philosophy and music. He taught them to ride, to shoot, to dance and to tell the truth. However, above all Chiron understood that there were more important things than knowledge or personal achievement. He ultimately gave his life in ransom for Prometheus so that mankind could have fire. He saw the greater good and it was within his power to secure it only at his own expense, yet he never hesitated. The word nobility is forever associated with Chiron.

The trend in Western Civilization over the last century has been toward emphasis on independence and isolation. However, given the growing interconnectedness of our world, much new thought has returned to the ideas of the primacy of interdependence over independence. This is good. We are going back to our origins. We can see it as a characteristic of our evolution that we are a communal species that has been dependent on one another for survival and self-actualization. It is only recently, historically speaking, that we have adopted the idea that we are an individual nuclear unit. However, as we grow older, this old wisdom of interdependence becomes more obviously true. We are now realizing that we are dependent on one another for the full realization of our potential as humans, because as step into our second adulthood, it will be defined by our relationships to others. If we live long enough, we cannot escape this fact. We can either exult in our interdependence or bemoan it. We can either commit to increase it or decrease it. I believe this is the role of the new elder. To step out of ourselves and into "the world" as a person committed to being of service to the larger community, the greater purpose. We can all then step into the universal truth, with the apostle Paul, we are "members of one another." We let go of control. We let go of the illusion of control.

OTHER MEN

I remember being all excited about a new business opportunity I was planning. I was feeling the necessity of it in response to some financial insecurity. I was sharing the idea with two of my closest male friends over dinner one night. They just listened. They did ask one question, "Have you committed to this yet?" The three of us had known each other for fifteen years. We had shared our ups and downs, our heart breaks and our triumphs. They had sat silently with me when I cried uncontrollably after my youngest daughter was diagnosed with schizophrenia. I had seen them through their divorces. We knew each other well at the core. I remember a night when two of us were leaving the hospital at 2 AM, after a very long and stressful day. As we passed in the hall, my friend just stopped. He stood silently. I waited. Finally, he simply said, "June asked for a divorce." He had never seen it coming. It was out of the blue. When a man tells another man such a thing, it has to be someone he deeply trusts because he doesn't know what he is going to do after the words come out.

Some few days after our above mentioned dinner conversation I got a call from one of them and he worked into the conversation that I had been the topic of conversation among my three closest friends (all male) and that they were very concerned about my new proposed venture. I went on to hear a thorough analysis of my business proposal and why it wasn't right for me. My friend carefully explained to me that while I had a lot to offer, I was least of all a businessman, and my proposed new venture would likely lead to not only the further undermining of my financial future but my emotional well-being as well. Within thirty minutes I was convinced. I slept on it and the next day thanked each one for saving me from myself. Their response was, "We know you. We couldn't let you do it." I thank my lucky stars for friends like these. I would literally give my life for any one of them.

We can not do this alone. We evolved to work in groups. We learned to trust each other by working and being together. Today's man is expected to go home and be happy with the wife and kids after working all day in a cubicle. This is unnatural. We need other men. Love is not a word we use easily with each other but, love it is. Life is good when you have a few men friends that know and care enough to save you from yourself.

TRANSFORMATION

We now know that we can do away with the concept of adulthood being one, long, stable, predictable period. We know that mid-life calls for an intentional reinterpretation of what is important in our lives. When American astronaut Buzz Aldrin set foot on the moon, he achieved his life's ambition. A former combat pilot and holder of a doctorate from MIT, he was as tough and as smart as they come. "All meat and stone," Norman Mailer wrote. But after he returned to earth, he became depressed, confused, and tearful. After achieving what he called "the most important goal of all," he finally confronted himself: "I had gone to the moon. What to do next? What possible goal could I add now? There simply wasn't one. I was suffering from what poets described as the melancholy of all things done." In his depression, his marriage unraveled and he began to drink. He took antidepressant medications and sought help form psychotherapy. "My depression forced me, at the age of forty-one, to stop and for the first time examine my life. I had conquered outer space but had no idea how to deal with inner space. The circumstances were extreme, but I now look upon this experience as one of the most valuable things I have ever done. It taught me to live again, at an age when it is very possible to begin anew."

Mid-life is, in fact, a time of natural transformation – metamorphosis. Up until now I have been emphasizing how we have been created for the first half of our lives – as hunters and warriors – and need to find a way of relating to our "planned obsolescence." But just maybe, this is not true. Maybe the Divine Process has planned way ahead for the human race. Maybe we are designed, having outgrown our original usefulness, to undergo a tumultuous transformation after forty-five. Maybe this transformation is not just for our own good but for the good of the world. Maybe this longevity that we are now experiencing is just the thing that is needed to save the world! Maybe we are the solution. The earth needs our wisdom. It needs men with time and intention to respond to the inequalities in our society and our abuse of the earth and each other. It needs men with the commitment to help one another.

We are growing older. How we feel about that process of aging profoundly influences our experience of our lives. Is aging a blessing or a curse? A decline or an ascent? An enemy or a guide? Our answer to these questions is important because in the second have of life, they shape our destiny. Hating aging becomes self-hatred. Age is not the enemy. The enemies are lovelessness, lack of compassion, emptiness, and self-absorption. So, what shall we do? How do we implement this "attitude adjustment?"

We reframe our "crisis" into a quest. Hope, promise, and meaning, are in the reframing. Maybe we were destined to go through a mid-life crisis. Maybe the world needs us to show the path to a new way of being, as elders. For what are we questing? We are on a quest for authenticity, integrity. In the second half of life, our old compass no longer works. The magnetic fields have altered. The new compass we need cannot be held in our hand, only in our heart. There are many "experts" who would map our future. Their maps are theirs. You may want to find your own map. Mid-life has befallen us. We did not ask for it. Mid-life transformation is part of our human heritage. We quest for meaning and transcendence - transcendence of our selves as the center of our universe - transcendence of our personal outcomes as the meaning of our lives. We want to be who we are inside, rather than who we appear on the outside. Have you ever heard of anyone upon their deathbed who said: "If only I had specialized more narrowly in my field?" Have you ever heard of a last will and testament in which the deceased said they wished they had not made love such a high priority; that they had not spent so much time with their children; or that they had not taken such good care of their health? Have you ever heard reports of wise elders who, looking back upon their lives, said they wished they had spent more time in the office; paid more attention to other people's expectations of them; or been more cautious in exploring new parts of themselves?

We never hear such regrets because the second half of life is a quest for wholeness. It turns the tables on the first half. It weights the balances in favor of integrity, interconnectedness, and interdependence. It asks us not to defend who we are but to be open to the mystery of what we have not yet become. We are coming into our own. Up until now, our goal has been to transcend the Warrior, the Wild Man, and become a King. A King over our own lives, a wise ruler over what we can influence and how we choose to live our lives. But now we aspire to go beyond sovereignty. We aspire to become the Sage, the Magician, and the Fool.

Any man who becomes comfortable with his own aging, is becoming comfortable with his own death. Becoming comfortable with one's mortality is like having a near death experience. Those that have undergone this experience, universally are found to have a different perspective on what is important. Their lives are changed. Their plans are changed. They go about their lives in a different way, seeking a more universal, transcendent meaning to their lives. They live with the knowledge that there is something greater than themselves out there, something greater than their own little mind seeking itself and its gratification. Having begun this transition then, we naturally take on these new roles.

The Sage's goal is to find out the Truth. He wants to understand and then live it. He is Socrates, standing in the square, in the middle of a circle of students. He is Jesus in the temple at twelve. The Sage's role is as the watcher, observing what is going on and exploring for Truth. His goal is to seek the absolute. Sufis teach us that understanding the ultimate Truth is not necessarily "far off or complicated." It only seems that way because people are so blinded by their preconceptions of the need for struggle, action and triumph. The quest is not just finding the ultimate Truth and finding it's availability in every day life and our capacity to take it in – to live it – to surrender to its reality. That is when knowledge becomes truthfulness. That is when knowledge becomes wisdom. That is when seeking becomes teaching in every moment. We pass on to others the Truth, not by our words alone, but by our actions.

The goal of the Magician is the transformation of lesser into better, greater realities. It is to transform, to heal. The gift of the Magician is personal power of a different kind. He is a bridge between the world grounded in the present moment and the transcendent meaning of the cosmos. He mirrors and illustrates that what we do in this moment affects all that there is and will be. He brings to bear, through ritual and invocation, the meaning of the consequences of our actions. He reframes perceptions. He consciously uses his knowledge that everything is interconnected. He demonstrates mastery. He reinterprets physical realities into mental, emotional and spiritual ones.

Finally, the Fool, or the Trickster, is the hardest role of all for some of us to assume. It is Thoreau, skipping and hopping in pirouettes on his skates. It is the man full of "aliveness," enjoyment and pleasure. We trust in the Process. We enjoy the journey for its own sake. Joy, freedom and liberation are the fruits of this role. Our society does not embrace this role. Eccentricity is not encouraged. The Fool on the other hand, delights in breaking the rules. "If I can't dance, I don't want to be part of your revolution," the Fool says. But the Fool has even another role, that of the Trickster for Truth. Like Don Juan, the great shaman of Carlos Castaneda's initiation novels, who literally tricks Castaneda into seeing the world from a different, altered perspective, most great teachers have learned to trick their students into wanting to learn. The Fool needs to be egoless, self-effacing, lest he be taken seriously and executed when he says to the King what needs to be said. Like the court Fools of Shakespeare, under the guise of frivolity and entertainment, he can say things to the "Rulers" that might get anyone else hanged. He is authentic. He operates behind a veil of egolessness. Life is good for the Fool. But he is not just about himself. He has found the joy of life in every moment, having gained some joint custody of his life with the transcendent. But he, like the Magician and the Sage, still has one foot grounded in the reality of the here and now and can impart tremendous perspective and wisdom to those of us still trapped in ourselves. So our ultimate goal is not one of earthly power. It is power of a different kind. The power to impact, transform and be of service to mankind – not as a CEO, although we may be one – but as a facilitator of transformation.

As we seek paths toward the sacred, the transcendent, they eventually lead us home. Whenever the spirit comes alive in us, in the second half of life, a commitment to serve emerges. One can view this psychologically and call it "generativity", as Erik Erickson does, or "charity" as Christianity does, or "seva" as Buddhists do. Whatever the cause, service is the path toward the sacred masculine second half. It is the path of integrity, leading to authenticity and awareness of Being something greater than ourselves. We are being called Home. We do not know by whom, or to where. But that, after all, is our quest. We have lived for self, now let us live for others. I believe we are being called to co-create today and tomorrow. Without our help, the world will not flourish. Don't wait for a Sage, Magician or Trickster to take your hand. Dare to become one.

> *"You don't give a weapon to a man until you've taught him how to dance."*
>
> —*Ancient Celtic Proverb*